THE YOUNG CRICKETER

Foreword by
ALEC STEWART

Bowling shoes

Batting gloves

Off-spin bowling

Wicket-keeping position

The backswing – preparing to hit the ball

Coaching ball

DK

DORLING KINDERSLEY
London • New Delhi • New York • Moscow • Sydney
www.dk.com

A DORLING KINDERSLEY BOOK
www.dk.com

Project Editor Indira Chandrasekhar

Project Art Editor Alpana Khare

Project Consultants Ian Gould, Phil Knappett, Unmish Parthasarathi

Photography Akhil Bakhshi, Steve Gorton

Photography coordination Radhika Singh

Art Editor Meera Handa

The young cricket players
Ishaan Singh Ahluwalia, Ishan Bakshi, Alex Brennan, Jack Deardon,
Sabir Gargouri Geels, Joshua Knappett, Manish, Sailesh Nagar,
Rakshit Pant, Toby Roland-Jones, Christopher Rossington, Liam Sampson,
Ronak Sekhri, N. Sheshadri, Vijay Victor, Amy Vincent

Additional staff
Project Editor Joanna Buck
Project Art Editor Jane Tetzlaff; **Editor** Ben Morgan
DTP Designer Almudena Díaz
Picture Research Mollie Gillard
Production Lisa Moss

First published in Great Britain in 1999 by
Dorling Kindersley Limited
9 Henrietta Street, London WC2E 8PS

Paperback edition 1999
2 4 6 8 10 9 7 5 3 1

Copyright © 1999 Dorling Kindersley Limited

All rights reserved. No part of this publication may be reproduced, stored in a retrieval system,
or transmitted in any form or by any means, electronic, mechanical, photocopying, recording,
or otherwise, without the prior written permisson of the copyright owner.

A CIP catalogue for this book is available from the British Library.

ISBN 0 7513 5831 2

Colour reproduction by Mullis Morgan, UK
Printed and bound by Graphicom, Italy

Contents

4
To all young players

5
History of cricket

6
What you will need

8
Preparing to play

10
What is cricket?

12
Rules of the game

14
Preparing to bat

16
Defensive strokes

18
Driving the ball

20
The on drive and sweep

22
The square cut

24
The hook, pull, and flick

26
Bowling basics

28
Swing bowling

30
The leg spin

32
The off-spin

34
Wicket-keeping

36
Fielding basics

38
Fielding activities

40
Taking it further

42
Tournaments and competitions

44
Glossary

47
Useful addresses

48
Index and acknowledgments

INTRODUCTION

To all young players

"*The game offers moments of excitement and despair for all players!*"

"I STARTED PLAYING CRICKET as soon as I could hold a bat. The game has been very good to me. It has given me the opportunity to play for and captain my country – the highest honour I could have achieved – as well as travel all around the world. However, I could never have reached the top of my profession without dedicated practice and lots of hard work. Like any player, I had to learn the basics first. This book will show you how to do just that!"

Game plan
Alec Stewart directs the field in his first game as England's captain, in 1998. Superb batting and wicket-keeping skills have made Alec a household name in the cricket world.

Master batsman
Ajay Jadeja is captain of the Haryana team in northern India and vice-captain of the Indian team. His superb batting skills have made him famous on the international scene as well as at home.

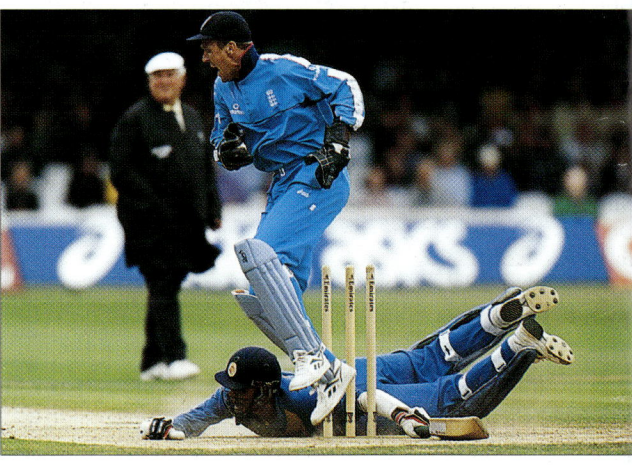

"*Batting can be the most demanding and exhilarating part of cricket.*"

"*Cricket is great fun and keeps you fit and healthy. Expect the unexpected as each new over is bowled.*"

4

History of cricket

CRICKET BEGAN in the English countryside. It dates back to the 14th century, when a distant cousin of the game – called 'Creag' – was played. From the 17th century onwards, a game more like modern cricket is mentioned consistently in local records. During England's colonial history, cricket spread to other countries, such as India, Australia, and South Africa. Although still considered an English pastime, cricket is now a major international sport enjoyed by millions of spectators worldwide.

Dr W. G. Grace
William Gilbert Grace (1848–1915) is the father of modern cricket. A cricket genius, he was the first player to score 1000 runs in one season. He forced bowlers to invent spins, swings, and overarm bowling to challenge him. Grace was probably the most popular sportsman of his time.

Donald Bradman
Australian legend Sir Donald Bradman (b. 1908) was the most successful batter in cricket history. He needed just 4 runs to retire from the game with a Test average of 100. He batted for the last time to a standing ovation, only to be bowled out with no runs. His final Test average was 99.94.

The early years
Cricket was enjoyed mainly by the English upper classes in its early years. A good cricket ground (such as Warwickshire in 1899, above) had a main playing field, a practice area, and a club house. The club house contained changing rooms for players and a bar for guests. The pitch was prepared by the head groundsman, who was highly respected by club members, players, and spectators alike.

Bodyline
England captain Douglas Jardine devised an aggressive bowling strategy called bodyline during a match with Australia in 1931. The bowler pitched the ball so that it bounced towards the batter's head or chest. Up to seven fielders waited close by to catch deflected balls. The strategy won England the Ashes, but it caused a bitter controversy that led to a change in the laws of cricket.

One-day cricket
A new type of cricket began in 1975, when England hosted the first cricket World Cup. Unlike Test matches, World Cup matches were, and still are, played in a single day, with each side taking only one turn to bat. The first World Cup was won by the West Indies, captained by Clive Lloyd (right). They defeated Australia by a narrow margin of 17 runs.

STARTING OUT

What you will need

ALL YOU NEED to play cricket is a bat and a ball. However, as you become more experienced you may want to join a cricket club and play in a team. Once you start to use a hard ball then you should make sure you have the necessary safety equipment. Wearing the correct cricket kit can make a big difference to your performance, and most importantly, help protect you from injury.

Junior cricket
This plastic cricket set is ideal for beginners. The lightweight bat and plastic ball make practising safe and fun for all ages.

Once you start playing in formal games you will need a wooden bat.

Tennis ball   Coaching ball   Junior ball

Cricket balls
In the early stages, it is a good idea to practise bowling with tennis balls marked with a seam. You can then progress to bowling with hard coaching balls. These are half red and half white – the red side is polished. Leather junior cricket balls are used for formal practice games.

A standard junior cricket bat

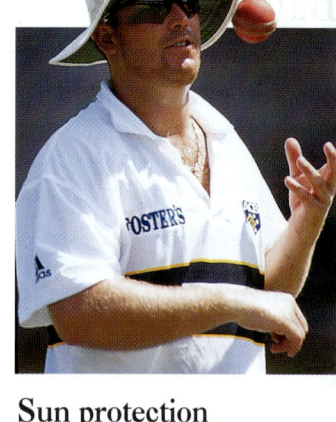

Sun protection
Australian leg-spin bowler Shane Warne is wearing the traditional floppy hat and sunglasses. It is advisable to wear sun-block as well as head and eye wear to protect you from the sun when playing outside.

Height of bat
It is important to choose a bat that is the right size and weight for you. Lean the bat against the outside of your leg. The top of the handle should reach the top of your thigh. If you can't lift the bat easily with one hand then it is too heavy.

Wicket-keeping equipment
Wicket-keepers spend most of the game crouched behind the stumps and bails (the wicket) ready to catch a speeding ball. It is important they wear the correct protective clothing – boys should wear a box.

A cap helps to shade the wicket-keeper's eyes.

Two wooden bails sit in grooves on top of the stumps.

The three wooden stumps are parallel to each other.

Inners
Inner gloves help absorb sweat, allow the wicket-keeper to grip the ball better, and cushion the impact on the hands.

Shoes
A comfortable pair of training shoes is all you need to start with. You may want to buy spiked shoes for playing outside when you are more experienced.

The gloves have thick padding and are webbed between the thumb and forefinger.

Wicket-keeping pads are wider and shorter than batting pads. They give added protection and mobility to the person behind the wicket.

WHAT YOU WILL NEED

Batting equipment

When using any type of hard ball, batters must wear batting pads and gloves, and boys should also wear a protective box. Helmets are optional, but are always a good idea, especially if you are facing a fast bowler. Girls can wear skirts or trousers.

The helmet should fit securely and comfortably.

The face mask allows you to see clearly and provides extra protection.

Wear your elbow guard on the arm facing the bowler.

A sleeveless or long-sleeved woollen pullover is useful in cold weather.

A cricket shirt should be comfortable and not restrict your arm movement.

The glove on your lower hand has extra protection for the thumb.

Batting pads should cover both legs above the knee. If they are too big it may hinder your batting strokes.

Three velcro straps hold the batting pads in place.

Make sure your shoes are the correct size.

Formal cricket
The traditional cricket dress for formal games is all white. However, players usually wear uniforms in solid team colours for one-day matches and night-cricket.

Most cricket bats are made of willow.

Optional equipment

Shoes
These shoes have rubber pimples on their soles, which are ideal for gripping the pitch in dry conditions. They can be used for batting, fielding, or bowling.

Velcro strap

Chest pad
It is a good idea to wear a chest pad when batting on a hard playing surface. It prevents injury to your ribcage.

Elbow guard
This is usually worn when batting against fast bowlers. It protects the forearm of the top hand.

Thigh pad
Thigh pads protect the area of the leg not covered by the batting pads.

Bowling shoes
A pair of spiked shoes is a wise investment for the serious fast bowler. The spikes grip the ground and prevent the bowler from slipping during run-up and delivery on wet pitches.

There are six spikes on the front of the shoe and four on the heel.

STARTING OUT

Preparing to play

IT IS ESSENTIAL to warm up and stretch before playing cricket, as this will reduce the risk of injury. You should loosen up your muscles by gentle jogging and doing some form of light mobility exercise before you start stretching. During the routine, keep your movements as smooth as possible and be careful not to overstretch. Hold each position for at least ten seconds. Don't forget to stretch again after you have played.

Keep your head level.

Elbow to knee
Place your hands behind your ears and raise the opposite knee to elbow, keeping your body straight.

Keep your arms straight and your head facing forwards.

Bend your supporting leg slightly.

Loosening up

Light mobility exercises, such as this arm rotation exercise, get the joints, muscles, and ligaments moving. They also increase the heart rate in preparation for your stretching routine.

Your legs should be slightly apart to help you balance.

Keep your hips and shoulders facing forwards.

Don't jerk your arms. Make the action one smooth, continuous movement.

1 Extend your right arm out in front and your left arm back as if you are swimming the front crawl. Keep your arms straight as they rotate in a forward circular motion.

2 Then rotate your arms in a backward circular motion, as if you are doing the back crawl.

Side stretch
This exercise is particularly important for bowlers. Stand with your feet shoulder-width apart. Raise your right hand above your head and slowly lean your body to the left, without leaning forwards or backwards. Repeat the stretch on the other side.

Keep your right arm straight.

Keep your back straight and your head upright.

Neck stretch

It's a good idea to start your stretching routine with your neck and work down the body. Whether you are batting, bowling, or wicket-keeping, the neck is under constant pressure. These exercises help prevent stiffness and improve flexibility.

Keep your shoulders down.

Be careful never to roll your head back.

1 Slowly move your head to the right. Feel the stretch on the left side of your neck.

2 Bring your head to the front. Feel a stretch in the back of your neck.

3 Let your head roll slowly to the left. Feel a stretch in the right side of your neck.

Shoulder stretch
Stand upright, with your feet shoulder-width apart. Try to touch your right shoulder blade with your right hand. Use your other hand to pull back gently on the bent elbow. Repeat with the left shoulder.

PREPARING TO PLAY

Calf stretch
Stand with one foot in front of the other, facing directly ahead. Lean forwards, making sure that your back heel stays on the ground. Push your body-weight forward until you feel the calf muscle stretching in your back leg. Repeat for the other leg.

Keep your back straight as you lunge forwards.

Bend your front knee and lean into the stretch.

Groin stretch
Sit on the ground with the soles of your feet together. Place your hands on your ankles and gently pull them in towards your body.

Keep your back straight.

Apply gentle pressure to your thighs with your arms.

Hamstring stretch
Lie on your back with your legs bent. Keeping your shoulders on the floor, gently pull your right leg up towards your chest. Feel the stretch in the back of your thigh. Repeat for the other leg.

Keep this leg slightly bent.

Thigh stretch
You may find it helpful to do this exercise leaning against a wall or with a partner to maintain your balance.

Make sure that your knees stay close together.

1. Hold the right ankle in your right hand. Stretch the front of the thigh by pulling your foot slowly backwards up to your bottom.

Increase each stretch when you feel the tension in your muscles releasing. Stretching should feel uncomfortable, but never painful.

Hold your left arm out to help you balance.

Your supporting knee should be slightly bent.

2. To increase the stretch, pull your foot in closer to the body. Repeat the exercise on the other leg.

Back stretches
1. Crouch down on the ground with your weight evenly distributed on your hands and knees. Keep your head up and your back flat.

Place your hands shoulder-width apart and facing forwards.

Keep your bottom pulled in tightly.

2. Tuck your head in and arch your back. You should feel a stretch in the upper back.

Push slowly on the bent leg to increase the stretch.

Lower back stretch
Sit on the ground with your legs straight out in front of you. Place the right leg over the left and twist your upper body in the opposite direction. Feel the stretch in the back of your thighs as well as the lower back. Repeat for the other side.

STARTING OUT

What is cricket?

CRICKET IS A GAME played between two teams, usually with eleven players on each side. The teams take it in turns to bat (take their innings) and field. The aim of the game is to score more runs than the opposition, before getting out (losing your wickets). Runs are scored by batters running between the wickets or hitting the ball over the boundary line. Cricket can be played on any size field with marked outer boundaries and a central strip known as the pitch.

Lord's Cricket Ground, London
The cricket ground at Lord's, which accommodates up to 30,000 people, is one of the best known in the world. The Marylebone Cricket Club (MCC), the club that owns the ground, and the English Cricket Board are located here. The MCC promotes and develops the game throughout the UK. The ground is used by junior cricketers as well as first-class players. Schools and clubs train in the indoor school and on the nursery ground.

The scoreboard
Scoreboards keep track of the batting and bowling scores and give details about runs scored and wickets taken. This electronic scoreboard shows that the batting team have scored 377 runs for 2 wickets (only two batters have been given out).

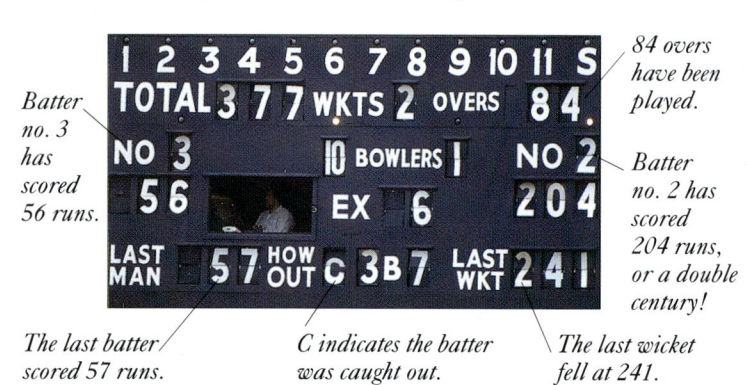

Batter no. 3 has scored 56 runs.

84 overs have been played.

Batter no. 2 has scored 204 runs, or a double century!

The last batter scored 57 runs.

C indicates the batter was caught out.

The last wicket fell at 241.

When off the field, players rest and watch the state of play from the dressing room or balcony.

An umpire

The sight screen is a large white surface made of wood or fabric that helps the batters to see the ball more easily.

The game

Batting order
Before the game begins, each captain writes down the batting order and gives the list to the umpire. However, the captain may change this order during a game.

The toss
The captains of both teams toss a coin in the presence of the umpire and the winner of the toss can choose to bat or field first.

Scoring runs
Batters score runs by running between the wickets after hitting the ball. If the ball travels across the boundary line, the batting side scores four runs automatically. If the ball crosses the boundary without bouncing on the outfield, they score six runs.

Extras
Extra runs can be scored when batters run without hitting the ball. These come from byes, leg byes, wides, or no-balls (see pages 12–13).

Bowling
There are usually four or more bowlers in a team. The bowler delivers six balls (an over) from one end of the pitch to the batter at the other end. Wide balls or no-balls do not count as part of the over. Another bowler delivers the next six balls from the opposite end of the pitch. No bowler is allowed more than one over at a time.

Fielding
The fielding side consists of a bowler, a wicket-keeper, and nine fielders. The fielders try to catch the batter out or retrieve the ball and return it to the wickets as fast as possible.

Duration
A team bats until ten batters are out, an agreed time limit is reached, or a certain number of overs have been bowled. The batting period is known as an innings. A match can be one or two innings long.

The officials
Two umpires enforce the rules of the game. One stands next to the bowler's wicket and the other stands on the leg side of the batter's wicket.

Substitutes
A substitute can be brought on only if a batter is injured and is unable to carry on playing. If an injured batter can still bat but cannot run, a runner is brought on.

WHAT IS CRICKET?

The playing field

Most of the action takes place on the pitch, which is usually in the centre of the field. The standard pitch is 20.12 m (22 yds) long and 2.64 m (8.8 ft) wide. The captain decides what positions fielders should take depending on the bowler's technique, the batter's strengths, and the conditions of the pitch. This diagram shows typical fielding positions for a junior game against a right-handed batter, but there are many possible variations to these positions.

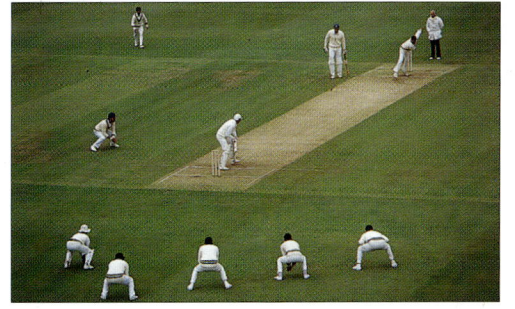

Close-in fielding

Here, close-in fielders are crouched in a ready position as the bowler delivers the ball in an international Test match. In a junior cricket game, there would not usually be as many fielders behind the wicket. In matches for players under 13 years old, fielders may not stand closer than 10 m (11 yds) from the batter's wicket.

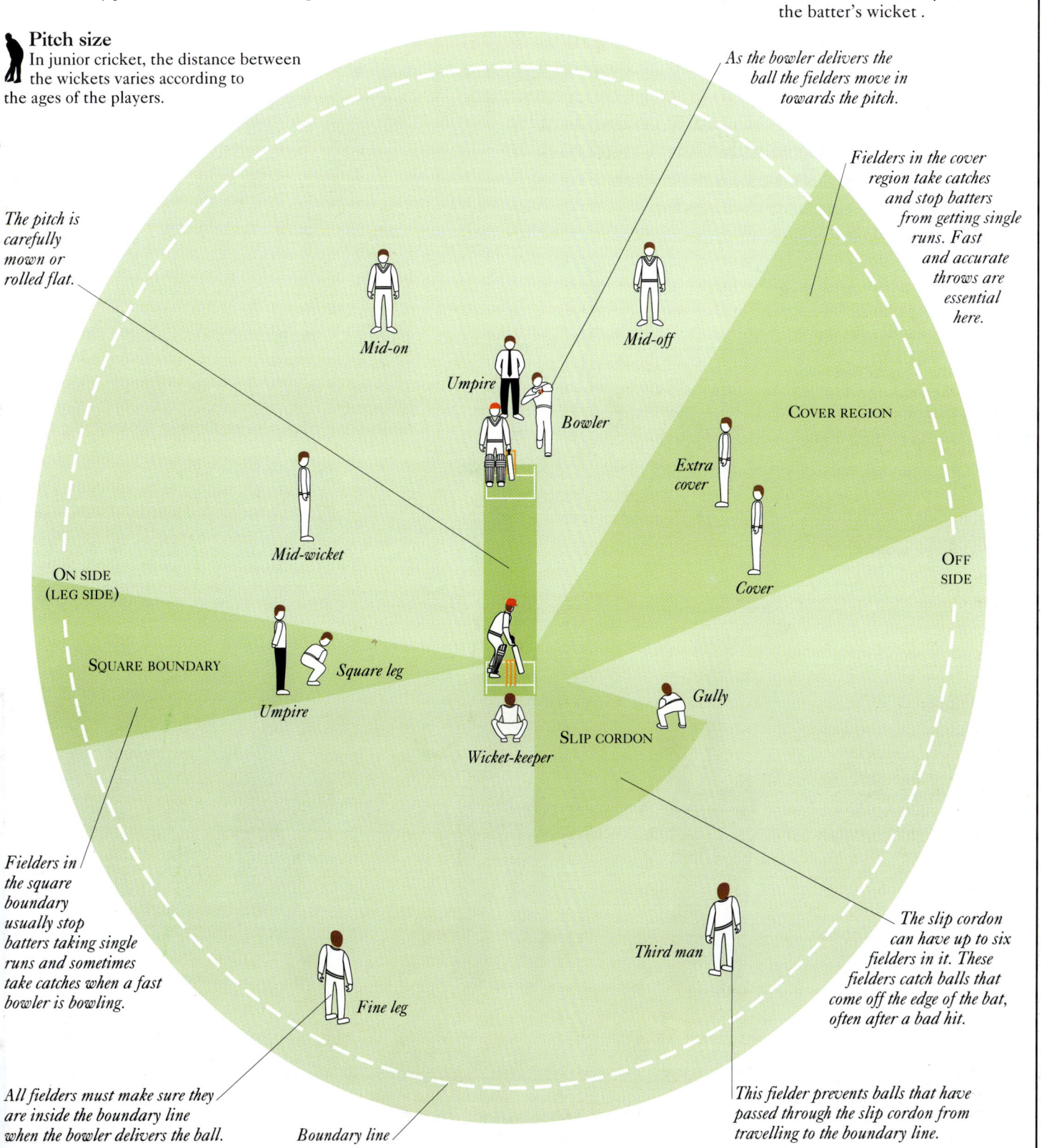

Pitch size
In junior cricket, the distance between the wickets varies according to the ages of the players.

The pitch is carefully mown or rolled flat.

As the bowler delivers the ball the fielders move in towards the pitch.

Fielders in the cover region take catches and stop batters from getting single runs. Fast and accurate throws are essential here.

- Mid-on
- Umpire
- Bowler
- Mid-off
- Extra cover
- COVER REGION
- Cover
- OFF SIDE
- Mid-wicket
- ON SIDE (LEG SIDE)
- SQUARE BOUNDARY
- Square leg
- Umpire
- Wicket-keeper
- SLIP CORDON
- Gully
- Third man
- Fine leg
- Boundary line

Fielders in the square boundary usually stop batters taking single runs and sometimes take catches when a fast bowler is bowling.

The slip cordon can have up to six fielders in it. These fielders catch balls that come off the edge of the bat, often after a bad hit.

This fielder prevents balls that have passed through the slip cordon from travelling to the boundary line.

All fielders must make sure they are inside the boundary line when the bowler delivers the ball.

STARTING OUT

Rules of the game

CRICKET MATCHES are governed by a strict set of rules that were drawn up over 250 years ago by a group of English noblemen. The rules cover every aspect of the game, from how batsmen are "given out" to the exact times of tea intervals. They are enforced by the umpires, who stand on the field and keep a close watch on the action. Cricket has evolved over the years, and from time to time the rules have changed. The rule book is kept by Marylebone Cricket Club, the sole authority able to change the rules, at Lord's Cricket Ground in London.

Ways of being out
When you are batting you are the focus of attention. The bowler leads the attack against you, assisted by fielders on their toes to take your wicket. If the fielding side think you are out, they will appeal to the umpire by shouting "Howzat?" If the umpire agrees, you are "given out" and must leave the pitch.

1. Bowled
You are bowled out when the bowler's ball hits the wicket and knocks off one or both bails ("breaks the wicket"). If the bails just wobble, you are not out.

The creases
Each end of the pitch is marked with white lines called creases that show where players can stand. The popping crease is the edge of the batter's safety zone – if you are outside it, you can be stumped or run out. This crease is also the line that must be reached to complete a run. The bowler must deliver the ball from between the return creases and is not allowed to step beyond the popping crease until the ball is released.

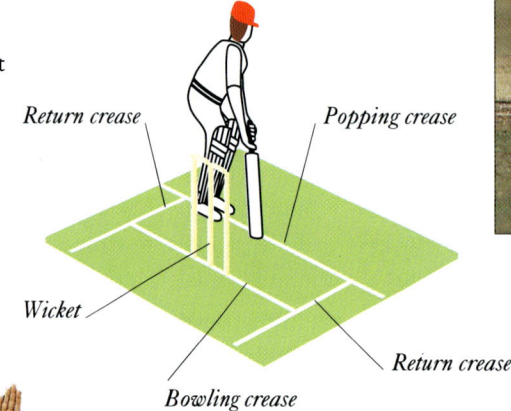

Return crease *Popping crease* *Wicket* *Return crease* *Bowling crease*

The umpires' signals

In official matches there are at least two umpires who make decisions about batting dismissals, the number of runs scored, and so on. The umpires use signals to make their decisions clear. They stand in two positions on the field. The stump umpire stands just behind the bowling crease. The square leg umpire stands in line with the popping crease, several metres behind the batter. Sometimes, a third umpire watches the match on a screen in the pavilion. The umpires can ask this umpire to decide on run outs, boundaries, stumping chances, and catches.

Bye
If the batter misses the ball and the ball also passes the wicket-keeper, the batter can run. A run scored this way is called a bye.

Four runs
If the ball is hit over the boundary and bounces on the way, the batter scores four runs. The umpire swings an arm horizontally.

Leg bye
If the batter's body accidentally deflects the ball during an attempt to bat, the batter can run. The run is called a leg bye.

Out
When the umpire raises an index finger in front of the head, the batter is out in one of the ten ways described above.

RULES OF THE GAME

2. Hitting the ball twice
If you hit the ball with the bat and then hit it again to score runs, you can be given out. However, you are allowed to use your foot or bat a second time to stop the ball from hitting the wicket, but you can't run.

3. Obstructing the field
You will be given out if you interfere with fielders while you are running. However, you may run in a path that blocks a fielder's throw. Obstructing the field can also mean insulting the umpires or other players.

4. Run out
You are run out if a fielder breaks the wicket nearest to you while you are running between the popping creases. The fielder can either throw the ball at the wicket or hit it with a hand holding the ball. If any part of your body or bat is inside the popping crease, you are safe.

5. Hit wicket
Be careful not to accidentally break the wicket while batting or taking off for a run, otherwise you will be out for hitting the wicket.

6. Timed out
If you do not come on to the field within two minutes of the previous batter's dismissal, you can be timed out.

7. Caught
If a fielder catches the ball after you have hit it and before it bounces, you are out. However, the fielder must not run on to the pitch or off the field to catch the ball. If the fielder steps over the boundary during the catch, you score a six.

The wicket-keeper has stumped out a batter who overstepped the crease and missed the ball.

The batter has been run out just before reaching the popping crease.

8. Stumped
If you miss a ball while batting and step outside the popping crease, the wicket-keeper will try to stump you out by catching the ball and breaking the wicket before you get back inside your crease.

9. Handled the ball
If you take a hand off the bat and touch the ball you will be given out, unless the fielding sides gives you special consent to touch the ball.

10. lbw
If you use your body to block a ball that would have hit the wicket, you can be given out lbw (leg before wicket). This can be difficult to decide and the umpire always has the final decision. Leg before wicket does not apply if the ball hits the bat first, or if the ball follows a very curved path and bounces outside the area

One-short
If a batter fails to step inside or ground the bat inside the popping crease at the end of a run, the umpire signals a one-short and the run does not count.

No-ball
If the bowler oversteps the popping or return crease, the umpire signals a no-ball. The batting side gets an extra run and an extra ball in the over.

Six runs
When the ball is hit beyond the boundary without bouncing first, the umpire awards six runs to the batting side by raising both arms in the air.

Wide
When the ball is pitched beyond the batter's reach, the umpire signals a wide. The batting side gets an extra run and an extra ball in the same over.

BATTING SKILLS

Preparing to bat

TO BE A SUCCESSFUL BATTER, you need good hand–eye co-ordination, sharp reflexes, and the confidence to make instant decisions on how to play a ball. You also need to master the basic techniques for batting. The correct grip, stance, and backlift are all important for developing a sound batting stroke. At first, get used to gripping the bat without gloves.

The grip
Grip the bat fairly firmly using both hands, not just the bottom hand. The correct grip allows both hands to work together effectively.

Hands out
Stand sideways-on to the bowler and rest the bat against your front thigh. Raise both hands to a horizontal position and then swing the hand nearest the bowler down to grip the upper section of the bat handle. Bring your other hand down to grip the bat below your top hand.

Your hands should be close together.

The V shapes should line up with each other.

Close up
Wrap your thumbs and forefingers around the bat handle to make two V shapes. The back of your top hand should always face the direction of the ball and both hands should be near the top of the bat handle. Practise this grip until it feels natural.

You should find your guard each time without looking at the wicket.

Middle stump

Leg stump

Off stump

Taking guard
You take a guard (mark a spot in the ground) to show you where to position yourself in front of the stumps each time you bat. Most beginners position their bats somewhere between middle and leg stump. The picture above shows a batter taking a middle-stump guard.

Left-handed batters
All batting instructions in this book are for right-handed batters. Try holding a mirror alongside these pictures to see the left-handed positions.

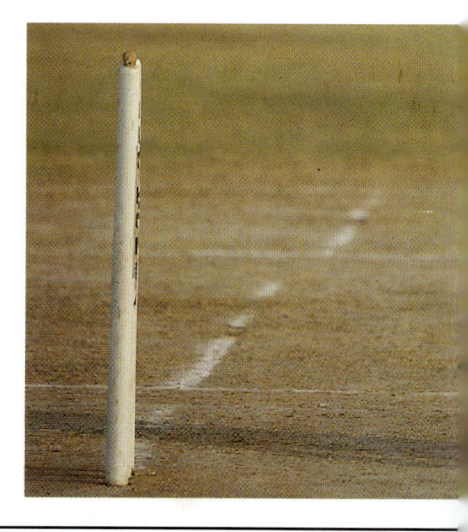

14

PREPARING TO BAT

The stance
The most important thing to remember about your stance is to be comfortable. You should feel relaxed, balanced, and ready to move quickly in any direction depending on the bowler's delivery.

Keep your hips and shoulders in line.

Try not to hunch your shoulders.

Ready position
Stand with your left shoulder pointing towards the bowler and your knees slightly bent. Your feet should be about a bat's width apart. Check your grip – your bat should be grounded just behind your back foot.

Your top hand lightly rests on the front batting pad.

Stand as tall as possible as you wait for the ball.

Raise the bat with the left hand, using the right for support.

On the pitch
Stand on the pitch sideways-on facing the opposite wicket. Place your feet either side of the popping crease. Your feet should be parallel to the crease and your weight distributed evenly. This will help you stay balanced and allow you to move quickly and easily.

Always wear gloves, pads, and a box if a hard ball is being used.

Take your time
Start your backswing in good time so that you get a smooth rhythm to your shot and don't have to rush.

The backswing
The backswing is the first movement of any stroke, when you raise your bat in preparation for hitting the ball. For a correct backswing, swing your bat straight back in line with the stumps, letting your top hand take control. Your left shoulder and elbow should point towards the ball.

Fix your eyes on the ball.

Keep your elbows clear of your body.

Keep your feet balanced and still throughout the action.

BATTING SKILLS

Defensive strokes

THE DEFENSIVE STROKES are crucial if you want to survive your first half hour at the crease. Practise them well and you will be able to fend off the best of bowling. Good defence not only increases your confidence, but also tires the bowler. Once you have settled in and gauged the pace and bounce of the ball, you can go on to play other strokes and the runs will begin to flow. Remember to keep your eyes on the ball, and always try to work out its "line" (direction) and "length" (the distance at which it pitches, or bounces).

Reaching out
Tall players like Australia's Tom Moody can reach a long way forwards when playing the forwards defence. This helps to counter spin and unexpected bounce. His back leg is straight and his body weight is on the front leg.

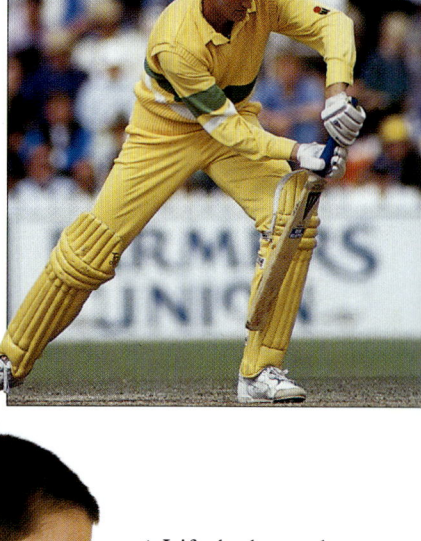

Make sure your head stays still when you lift the bat. Otherwise, you may misjudge the line and length of the ball while it is in the air.

Lift the bat straight up behind you.

1 Lift the bat early, mainly using the left hand. The right hand should only be used as support. Watch the ball as it leaves the bowler's hand, keeping your head still.

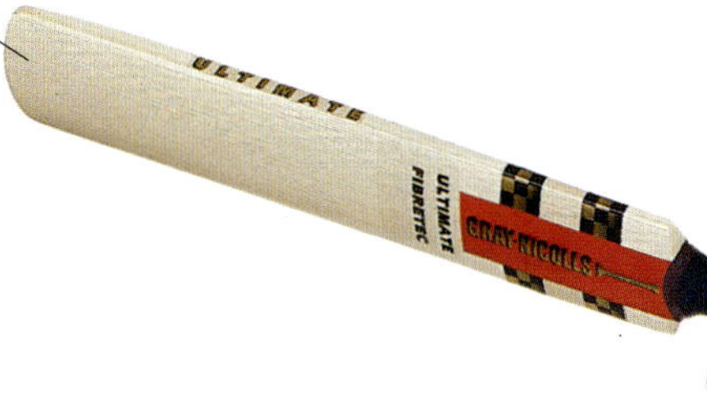

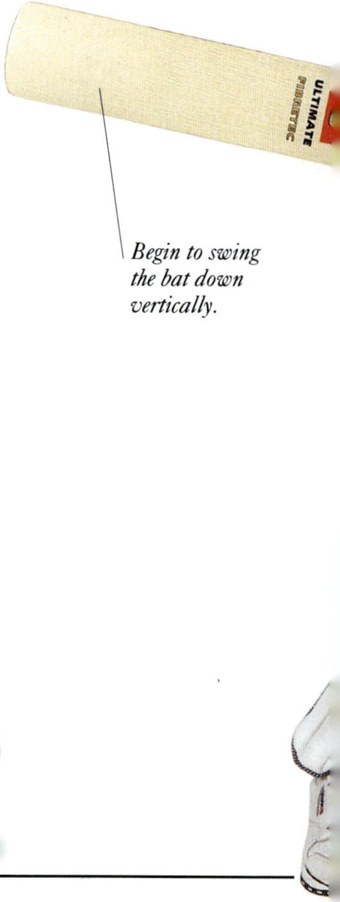

Your left shoulder should face the bowler.

Begin to swing the bat down vertically.

Forward defence

Good bowlers will try to get you out by pitching the ball up towards you. The forward defence is your best chance of keeping them at bay. Play this stroke to a ball that pitches in line with the wicket at a "good length" – a distance that makes it difficult to decide whether you should move forwards or backwards to hit the ball. Move your foot in line with the direction of the ball, and block it with the straight face of the bat.

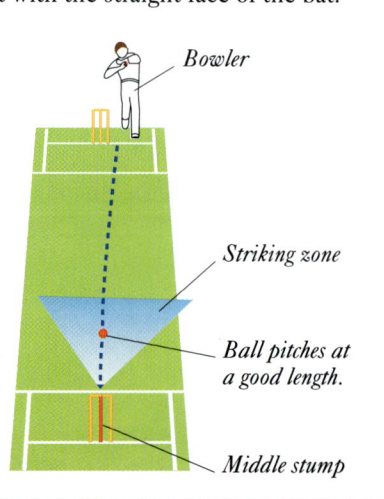

Bend your knees slightly as you wait for the ball.

Bowler

Striking zone

Ball pitches at a good length.

Middle stump

16

DEFENSIVE STROKES

Back-foot defence

Play this stroke instead of the forward defence to balls that pitch slightly shorter and bounce higher. Unlike the forward defence, this shot is played with the bat held high. The body should stay side-on during the shot.

Bowler

Ball pitches slightly shorter than a good length (short of a length).

Striking zone

Middle stump

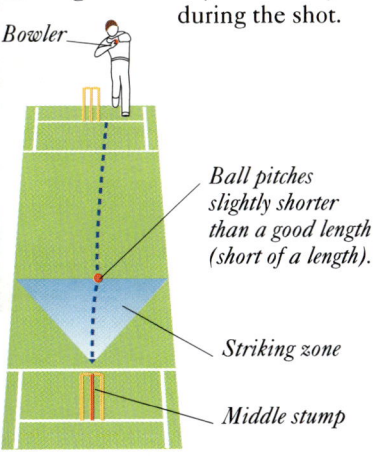

Guide the bat with the left hand, using the right hand as support.

Take your body weight on to the ball of your right foot.

Your body moves back, while your head stays forward.

Angle the bat downwards to keep the ball low.

Keep your right foot parallel to the crease.

1 Raise the bat, making sure the backswing is correct. Keeping your head still, watch the ball as it leaves the bowler's hand.

2 Once you have determined the line and length of the ball, move your right foot back just inside the line of the ball.

3 Bring the bat into a vertical position with your hands held high. Your weight should be evenly balanced with your head forward.

---

2 Lean towards the line of the ball, leading with your head and shoulder. Your left foot will step forwards automatically if you lean properly. Make sure your left hand remains in control of the bat as it begins to move down.

3 Bring the bat down so that it is angled downwards just in front of your left leg. Viewed from the front, there should be no gap between the bat and your front pad. Your left hand stays in control of the bat.

Aim to have your nose over the ball as it makes contact with the bat.

Keep your left knee forwards.

Straighten your back leg.

Take your body weight on your front foot.

The bat should show full face and be angled downwards to keep the ball low.

17

BATTING SKILLS

Driving the ball

CRICKETERS SAY that a batter who can't drive is only half a batter. Drives are not only the most important attacking strokes to learn, they are also the most exciting to play. They are most effective against balls that pitch close to the wicket, which you can strike just as they come off the ground. Depending on the line of the ball, you can either drive it straight ahead (straight drive), towards the off side (cover drive), or towards the on side (on drive). The first steps of a drive are like a forward defence, so you can switch between defence and attack at the last moment.

Best foot forwards
South African captain Hansie Cronje puts his best foot forwards to play a drive. Look at the position of his head – it has stayed down after playing the shot.

The cover drive

This is one of the most elegant strokes that a batter can play. Play it to balls pitching in line with or just outside the off stump. As with all drives, it is crucial to lean your whole body forwards into the line of the ball, leading with your head and shoulder. As you do so, you will step forwards automatically. Strike the ball as late and as close to your body as possible.

1 Raise the bat, making sure you have the correct backswing. Keep your head still and determine the line and length of the ball as it leaves the bowler's hand.

Keep your eyes on the ball.

2 Lean towards the ball, leading with your head and left shoulder. Keep your bat high until your body weight has begun to transfer forwards on to your left foot.

Aim your left shoulder and h[ead] in the direction [of] the oncoming b[all].

Bowler

Ball pitches close to crease (full length or half volley).

Striking zone

Off stump

Bending your knees a little helps you move quickly against fast bowling.

Transfer your body weight on to your left foot.

Transfer your body weight from the heels to the toes as you lift the bat to play the shot.

DRIVING THE BALL

The straight drive

This powerful attack stroke sends the ball directly back towards the bowler. Play the straight drive to a full-length ball pitching in line with the off and middle stumps. A correct backswing that brings the bat down straight past the left pad is very important.

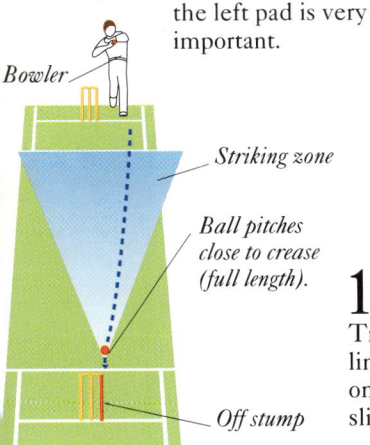

Bowler

Striking zone

Ball pitches close to crease (full length).

Off stump

Lift the bat straight up behind your head.

Lean into the line of the ball, leading with head and left shoulder.

If your right elbow stays close to the body, the bat will come down straight.

The bat should graze the inside of your left foot.

Play the shot with the full face of the bat.

The bottom hand carries the weight of the bat upwards.

1 Raise the bat and keep your head still. Try to determine the line and length of the oncoming ball. Bend slightly at the knees.

2 Lean towards the ball and move your left foot to near where it will pitch. Your backswing should be at the top by this stage.

3 Bring the bat down vertically, accelerating it as you make contact. Your body weight should be on your front foot.

4 Follow through and finish with your hands high. Keep your eyes on the ball and look for an opportunity to run.

Watch the ball as it hits the ground and adjust to last-minute changes in direction and bounce.

3 With your weight on the front foot, swing the bat down vertically to hit the ball just after it pitches. Keep your head steady and your eyes on the ball as it hits the bat.

Make sure you look down rather than up. If your head stays down, so will the ball.

Position your front pad so that the ball is close to it when the bat makes contact.

4 Finish the shot with your hands high. At this point, you should be holding the bat equally with both hands. Your back leg should straighten out as you complete the stroke.

Playing the ball as late as possible helps you cope with late swing and seam movement, and improves your timing.

Body weight on front foot

BATTING SKILLS

The on drive and sweep

GOOD BOWLERS TRY TO PITCH the ball in line with the off stump. As a result, batters play most balls to the off side, so most of the fielders are positioned there too. The on drive and the sweep send the ball to the on side. With fewer fielders to beat, these strokes can bring lots of runs. Make sure you play these shots only to balls in line with or outside the leg stump.

Bowler

Striking zone

Ball pitches near crease (full length).

Leg stump

The on drive

This shot is useful for balls that pitch close to your feet, in line with or outside the leg stump. The technique is similar to the cover drive and straight drive, but you should not step out so far with your leading leg. The on drive is difficult – only the very best batters can play it properly.

1 Raise the bat early when facing fast bowlers, and make sure your backswing is correct. By the time the ball reaches the middle of the pitch, you should have determined its line and length.

If you play the on drive to a ball pitching on the middle and off stumps, you are very likely to be given out leg before wicket.

Keep your left shoulder low.

2 Lean into the line of the ball, leading with your head and left shoulder, and step forwards with your left foot. Bring the bat vertically down to hit the ball just after it pitches.

Hit the ball with a straight bat.

Keep your knees slightly bent.

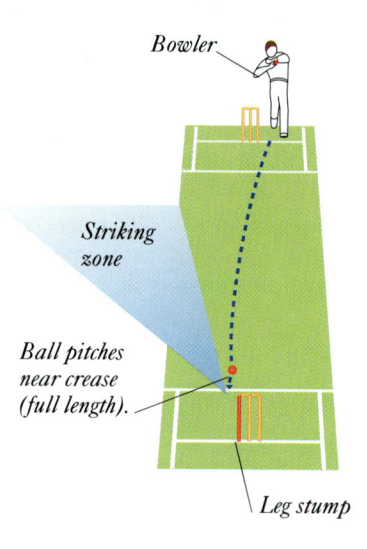

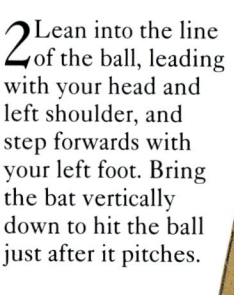

Your front leg should take your body weight.

3 As you follow through, your body should turn anticlockwise. Your right shoulder should be visible to the umpire when you complete the shot.

20

THE ON DRIVE AND SWEEP

The sweep
Unlike the on drive, the sweep is played with a horizontal movement of the bat. The bat should sweep around your body to your left, sending the ball squarely on to the leg side or behind the wicket. Play this stroke to good length balls that pitch in line with or outside the leg stump. The initial movements of the sweep are similar to the forward defensive.

Keep your eyes on the ball and try to work out its line and length.

Take the weight of the bat with your left arm. Use the right arm for support.

Bowler

Ball pitches at good length.

Striking zone

Leg stump

Timing is important. Trying to hit the ball too hard might not allow you to roll your wrists around at the right time.

Clean sweep
Australia's Steve Waugh often uses the sweep to smother a spinner's challenge. Watch how he stays perfectly balanced after playing the shot.

1 Lift the bat straight up behind you. Lean forwards and step towards the line of the ball as it pitches.

2 Swing the bat horizontally to make contact with the ball in front of you just after it pitches. The ball should hit your pad if it misses the bat.

Your right knee should come down towards the ground.

Look for a chance to run.

Turn your wrists anticlockwise as you follow through.

3 Watch the ball make contact with the bat. Bend your front leg completely, allowing the back leg to trail. Roll your wrists anticlockwise so that the bat doesn't fly out of your hands.

BATTING SKILLS

The square cut

THE SQUARE CUT and back-foot attack are played to balls that pitch a long way in front of the batter (short deliveries), on or outside the off stump. The back-foot attack is played with the full face of the bat, sending the ball in front of the stumps towards the cover region. The square cut deflects the ball towards the off side at right angles to the pitch, or "square".

Eyes on the ball
Australia's Mark Waugh plays an expert square cut. He has just hit the ball (between stage 4 and 5 below). His eyes are still fixed on the point of contact.

Looking at the approaching ball over your left shoulder will help you stay side-on.

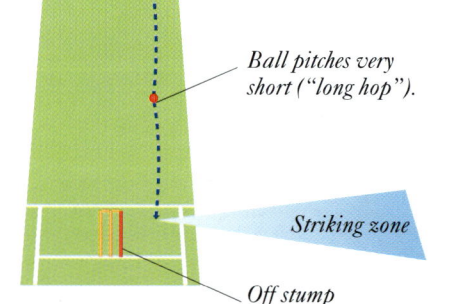

Lift the bat straight up behind your head.

Turn your front shoulder towards the off side.

The square cut
This is a difficult shot so you should practise it as much as possible before trying it out in the field. Unlike the back-foot attack, the square cut is usually not played to a ball in line with the stumps. It is safer to play it to a ball pitching wide of the off stump. The toes of your right foot should stay parallel to the stumps.

Flex your knee.

Bowler

Ball pitches very short ("long hop").

Striking zone

Off stump

1 Lift the bat and watch the ball to work out its line and where it will pitch. Keep your left shoulder pointing towards it.

2 Move your right foot across towards the line of the ball. The foot should be parallel to the stumps with toes pointing to the off side.

THE SQUARE CUT

The back-foot attack

Play the back-foot attack to short balls that pitch just outside the off stump and bounce bail high. It is important to know exactly where your off stump is as this will help you decide how far to move your back leg. This shot can earn you runs if the ball is played successfully through a gap between fielders on the off side.

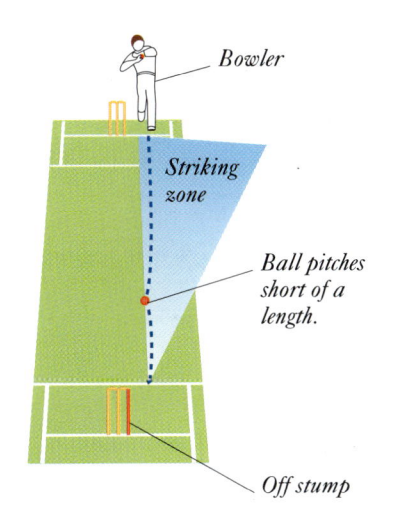

Bowler

Striking zone

Ball pitches short of a length.

Off stump

Watch the approaching ball from over your left shoulder.

Keep your head steady and forwards.

Step forwards on to your back foot.

1 Ensure a correct backlift and watch the ball to work out its line and length. Keeps your knees slightly flexed.

2 Move your right foot towards the stumps and in line with the ball. Keep it parallel to the crease.

3 Your left elbow should be high as you make contact. The left hand controls the bat, the right hand "punches".

Head steady

Keep your eyes fixed on the ball.

Arms extended

The right shoulder will be revealed more when the square cut is played to a ball pitching on the off stump and coming into your body.

3 Swing the bat from high to low with your arms extended and the bat horizontal. Your right hand should control the stroke.

4 Transfer your weight to the right foot as you make contact with the ball. Keep you head steady and your eyes on the ball.

5 Follow through with your weight on the right foot. As you finish the shot, your head should stay still. Your hands and bat finish high.

23

BATTING SKILLS

The hook, pull, and flick

THE HOOK, PULL, AND FLICK send the ball on to the leg side, where there are fewer fielders. All these shots are played against balls that pitch in line with the middle and leg stumps. Your right foot should move backwards and across, depending on the line of the ball. The hook is played to a ball that pitches short and bounces up close to shoulder height. The pull is used when the ball pitches closer to you and bounces between your knee and hip. Play the flick (leg glance) if the bounce is unpredictable, or if you face spinners.

Perfect balance
Ajay Jadeja's upper body has pivoted on his right foot, while his head remains steady as he plays the perfect pull shot.

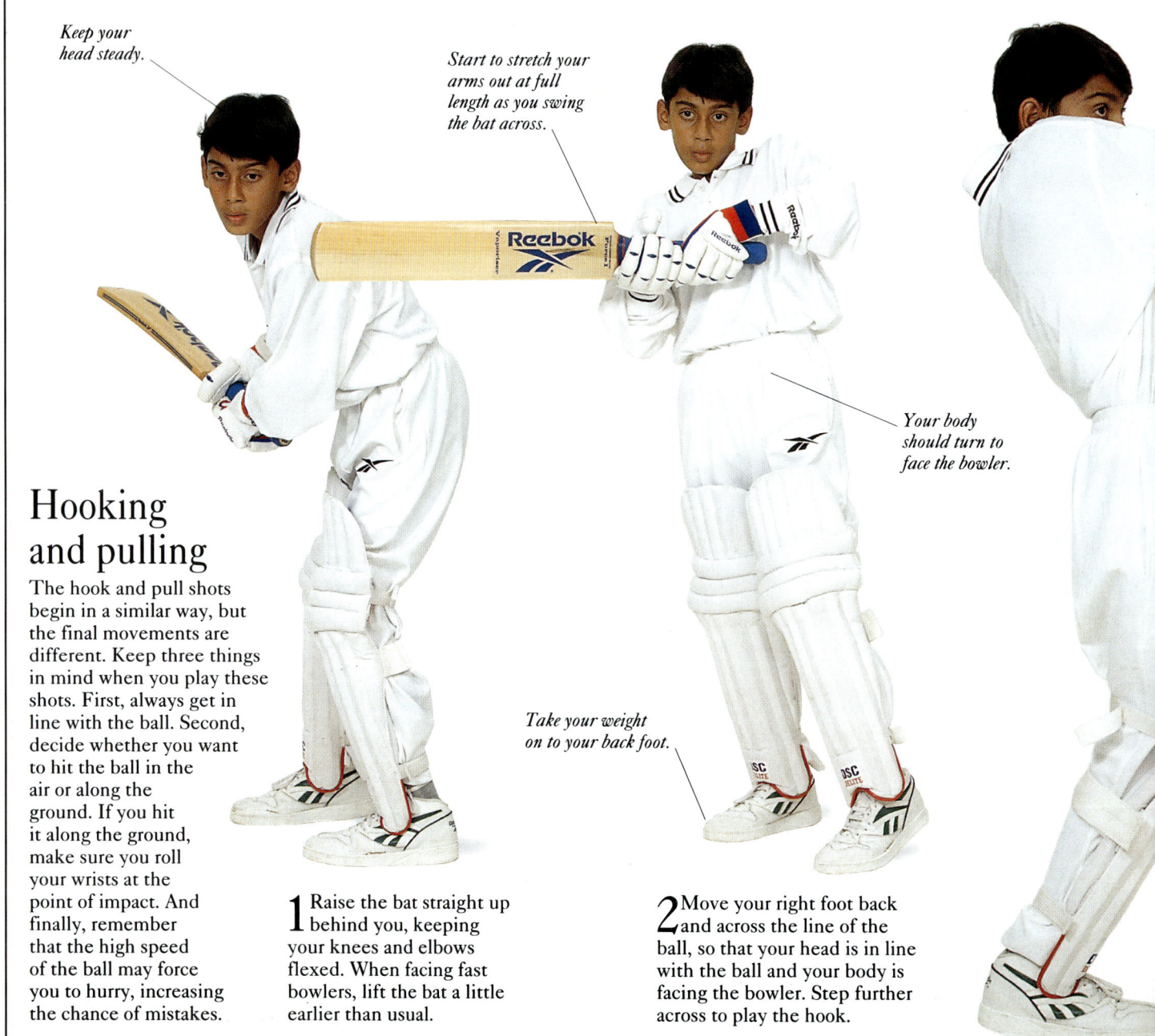

Keep your head steady.

Start to stretch your arms out at full length as you swing the bat across.

Your body should turn to face the bowler.

Hooking and pulling

The hook and pull shots begin in a similar way, but the final movements are different. Keep three things in mind when you play these shots. First, always get in line with the ball. Second, decide whether you want to hit the ball in the air or along the ground. If you hit it along the ground, make sure you roll your wrists at the point of impact. And finally, remember that the high speed of the ball may force you to hurry, increasing the chance of mistakes.

Take your weight on to your back foot.

1 Raise the bat straight up behind you, keeping your knees and elbows flexed. When facing fast bowlers, lift the bat a little earlier than usual.

2 Move your right foot back and across the line of the ball, so that your head is in line with the ball and your body is facing the bowler. Step further across to play the hook.

THE HOOK, PULL, AND FLICK

The leg glance or flick

This shot deflects balls behind the wicket and on to the leg side. The stroke demands timing and a soft touch because the ball needs to be deflected gently at the last moment. It is not an easy stroke, so make sure you practise thoroughly before trying it in a match. Avoid using it on wet or uneven pitches.

Bowler
Begin with a correct backlift.
Bounce
Striking zone
Leg stump

1 Move your right foot across and back (towards the stumps). Your right foot acts as a pivot as you turn to take the shot.

2 Watch the ball closely on pitching. Use your left hand to bring the bat down to make contact. Use your right hand to swivel the bat so that it deflects the ball behind you.

The bat should make contact just a few inches in front of your left leg.

Roll your wrists anticlockwise as you strike the ball.

Keep your head behind the line of the ball.

When playing the hook shot it is safest to wear a helmet.

Bowler
Ball pitches short and bounces high.
Leg stump
Striking zone

Bowler
Ball pitches short of a length.
Striking zone
Leg stump

3a The hook shot

For the hook, swing the bat horizontally across with your arms fully extended. Your whole body should rotate, pivoting on the right foot, so that you turn to face leg side. Roll your wrists to turn the bat down and keep the ball low, and be ready to duck if you don't hit the ball. Only attempt this shot if you are an experienced batter.

3b The pull shot

The pull is easier than the hook. As in the hook, the bat is swung horizontally across with your arms extended and your right foot acting as a pivot. However, your body should not rotate as much as in the hook. The ball is hit squarely to the leg side and down into the ground. At the end of the shot, your body weight transfers on to the left foot.

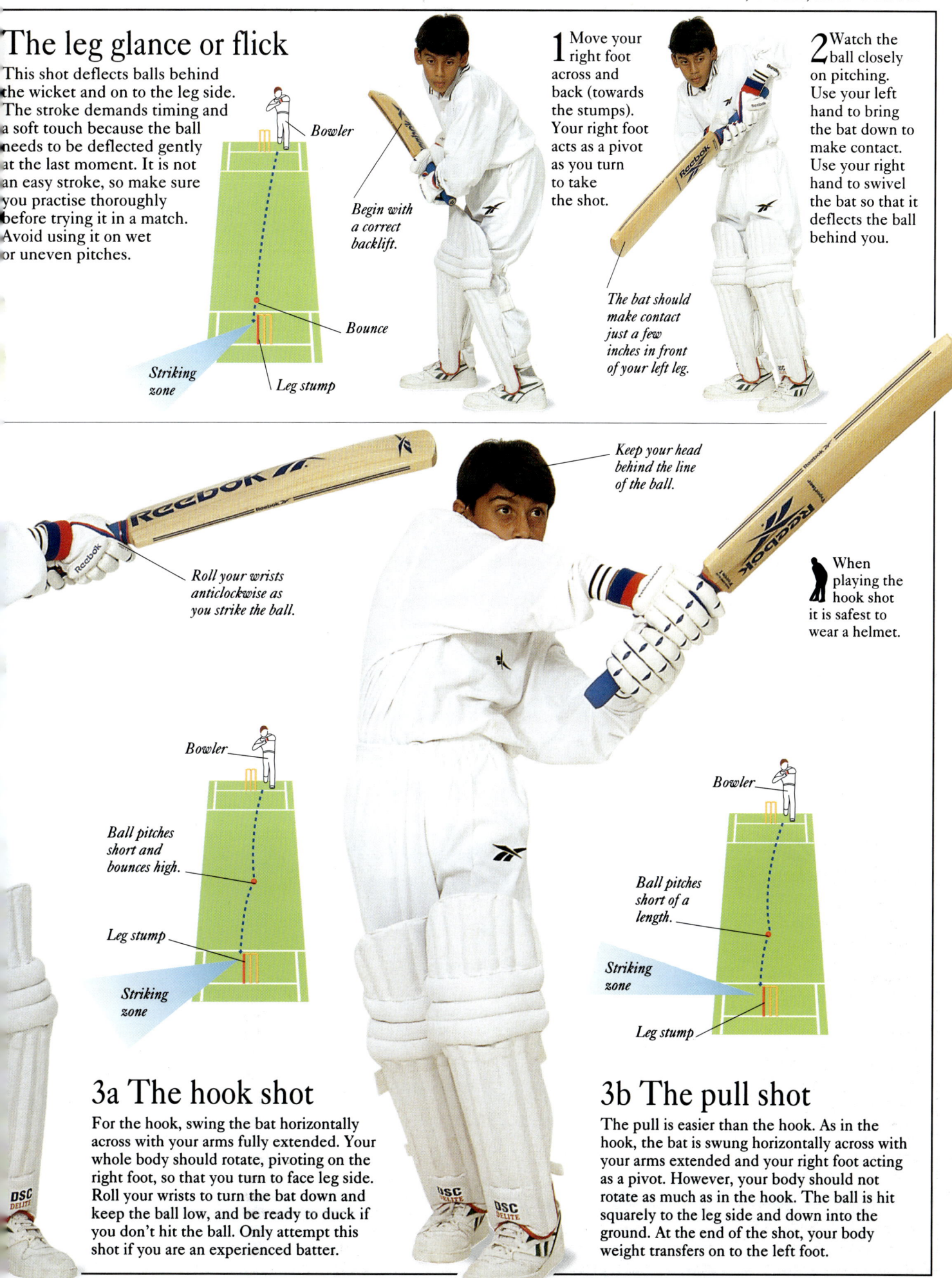

BOWLING SKILLS

Bowling basics

THERE ARE FOUR basic elements to bowling: the grip, the run-up, the delivery (stages 1, 2, and 3) and the follow-through (stages 4 and 5). You should aim to achieve a consistent, smooth run-up and an accurate delivery. Don't worry too much about speed to start with.

Pump your arms to help gain momentum as you run.

Long strides help you develop a good rhythm.

The bowling action

The bowling action starts at the end of the run-up and includes the delivery and follow-through. Beginners usually learn to bowl with a side-on action, which is demonstrated in this sequence.

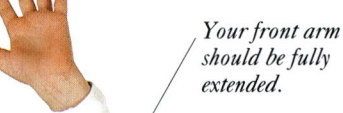

Your front arm should be fully extended.

Your bowling hand should be under your chin.

Keep your eyes on the wicket.

The run-up

The run-up usually consists of five to eleven paces for beginners. It is helpful to pace these out backwards from the bowling crease and mark the spot you start from. Keep practising your run-up so that it is consistent each time you bowl, and try to create a steady, smooth rhythm as you run.

Lean your upper body away from the batter.

1 Take off from your left foot and turn your body 90° in the air so that your left shoulder moves to face the batter. This is the start of the delivery.

Extend your front leg to help you balance and propel you forwards.

Your back foot should land parallel to the bowling crease.

Your weight moves from your left foot on to your right foot.

2 As you land on your right foot, you should be sideways-on to the opposite wicket. Bring your left hand high above your head. Look over your left arm towards the wicket.

BOWLING BASICS

The basic grip

The way that you hold the ball depends on the type of delivery you want. However, it is important to master the basic grip and bowling action before trying more advanced techniques. Hold the ball with the seam in a vertical position. Make sure you grip the ball with your fingers and not your palms.

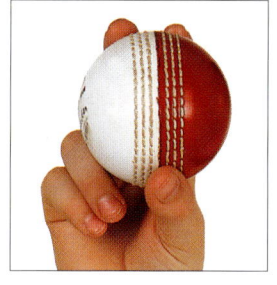

Place your middle and index fingers on either side of the seam. Your thumb should be directly underneath.

Turn the ball to the side to check there is a gap between the ball and the "V" of your thumb and index finger.

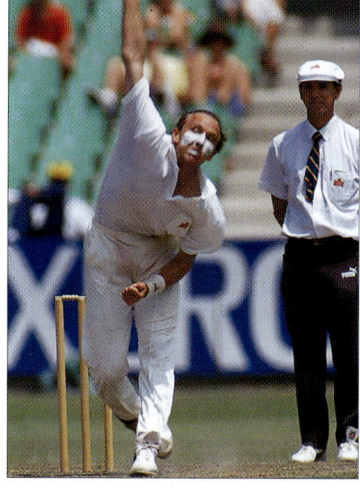

Fast bowling
South African bowler, Allan Donald, has a perfectly straight arm as he releases the ball and begins the follow-through. His body is perfectly balanced as he completes the action at high speed.

Left-handed bowlers
All bowling instructions in this book are for right-handed bowlers. Try holding a mirror alongside these pictures to see the left-handed positions.

Look at the wicket over your non-bowling arm.

Your bowling arm should be straight and your wrist cocked.

Don't let your chin drop after follow-through.

3 Transfer your weight on to your leading foot, bringing your front arm down and extending your bowling arm out behind you. Begin to turn your hips and shoulders to face the wicket.

Your hips should now be facing forwards.

4 Extend your bowling arm to its highest point and release the ball. This is the start of the follow-through. Keep your head and eyes level.

Keep your right knee in line with the ball.

Start to move your back leg towards the wicket.

5 Bring your bowling arm down across your body as you turn your right shoulder in an anticlockwise direction. Move your left arm backwards and upwards and keep your eyes fixed on the target. Keep your right knee close to your body.

BOWLING SKILLS

Swing bowling

SWING BOWLERS PLAY in such a way that the ball swings, or curves, in flight. This is a useful technique to master as it does not require fast bowling, yet batters find these balls difficult to play. The amount the ball swings depends on the angle of the ball's seam as it is released and how much shine is put on the ball. Inswing bowlers curve the ball in towards the batter, whereas outswing bowlers curve the ball away from the batter.

The inswinger

If bowled correctly, the inswinger will bounce close to the wicket, forcing the batter to hit the ball. Direct the ball towards the off stump to allow space for it to swing in flight. Your run-up should be straight, but aim to release the ball slightly wider on the crease than for an outswinger.

The inswing grip

Hold the ball with the seam vertical and angled towards fine leg. Your middle and index fingers should be fairly close together on either side of the seam, and the ball should rest on the flat of your thumb. Make sure the shiny side of the ball is facing the off-side.

1 As you approach the crease, you should be sideways on to the opposite wicket with your front arm held high. Keep your eyes on the target, looking inside your non-bowling arm.

Lean away from the batter.

Keep your hips and shoulders in line with each other.

2 Extend your bowling arm as high as you can, turning your body to face the opposite wicket. Pull your front arm down and close in to your body. Release the ball as it reaches its highest point.

Keep your hands and fingers behind the ball.

Keep your head straight and your eyes on the target.

Keep your left arm straight as you move it down.

Transfer your weight from your back leg to your front leg as you release the ball.

3 Keep your bowling arm straight and bring it down the right side of your body. Your shoulders should be facing forwards and your left arm moving backwards and upwards.

Keep your shoulders and hips in line.

A relaxed run-up and correct use of the left arm will help you stay balanced.

SWING BOWLING

The outswinger

When it swings late, the outswinger can dismiss even the best batter, who is given very little time to adjust to the change in direction. Direct the ball at the leg stump to give it space to curve in flight, and aim to pitch it fairly close to the wicket. If the ball is short and wide, the batter can score runs by playing the back foot attack or the square cut (see pages 22–23).

The outswing grip

Hold the ball with the seam vertical and angled towards first slip. Your middle and index fingers should be fairly close together on either side of the seam. The ball should rest on the side of your thumb and not on the flat part as for the inswinger. Make sure the shiny side of the ball is facing leg side.

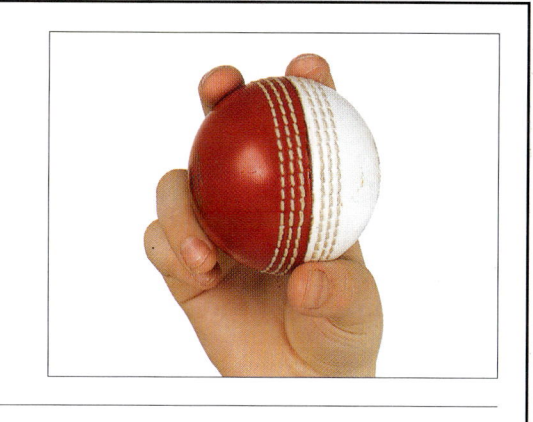

1 Look at the target over your non-bowling arm, keeping a sideways-on position. Place your back foot parallel to the crease.

2 Turn your body to face the wicket as you prepare to release the ball. Your bowling arm should extend upwards, but it does not need to be completely vertical.

3 Follow through vigorously, swinging your bowling arm across your body. Your shoulders and hips should face forwards. Keep your eyes fixed on the target.

Keep your eyes fixed on the target.

Lean slightly backwards.

A raised front leg will help propel you forwards.

Keep your wrist cocked until you release the ball.

Keep the chin up and your head straight as you follow the ball after it leaves your hand.

Your bowling arm should be straight.

Your left leg and bowling arm should be in line.

Transfer your weight to the left foot.

Swing your left arm back and up.

Rotate your shoulders in an anticlockwise direction.

Your right knee should stay close to your body.

29

BOWLING SKILLS

The leg spin

A LEG-SPIN BOWLER spins the ball so that it changes direction from the leg stump to the off stump after it pitches. Although a fairly slow ball, a leg spinner can dismiss the best of batters when bowled well. The leg spin is a difficult technique to master – as the ball is released, the bowler's wrist flips over towards the batter while the third finger spins the ball along the seam.

Leg-spin bowling

Leg-spin bowlers take a shorter run-up than fast bowlers. They run at a slight angle towards the popping crease to help them keep their sideways-on position. A leg spinner is an attacking style of bowling which can take a lot of wickets. However, if it is not bowled correctly, batters can easily score runs.

The leg-spin grip

Grip the ball by placing your first and second fingers across the seam at the top. Your third finger is bent and also lies along the seam. Try not to rest the ball on your thumb. Flick your wrist forwards as you release the ball, so your palm faces down.

1 Grip the ball with your first two fingers on top and your third finger bent along the seam. Make sure your palm is facing the batter. Move your bowling hand backwards past your hips. Lift your left arm, using it to balance the body, and look at the wicket from over your left shoulder.

Spin is achieved by rotating your wrists.

Keep looking forwards as you lean away from the batter.

Stand tall and keep your back straight.

To help you stand side-on, keep your back foot as parallel to the crease as possible.

2 Swing your bowling arm backwards and upwards, keeping it close to your right ear as your hand moves over your head. Transfer your weight on to your front foot, positioning your body slightly towards the leg stump.

30

THE LEG SPIN

Release the ball from as high a position as possible.

Use the left arm to balance the body as your weight moves forwards after delivering the ball.

Leg spin delivery
Here we can see Australian cricketer Shane Warne balance his body with his left arm as he prepares to deliver a leg-spin bowl. His balanced sideways-on position ensures a powerful body action.

Your head should be upright and steady.

Use your bowling arm to help give your follow-through momentum.

Keep your front knee steady.

Make sure your follow-through is energetic and powerful.

3 As you swing your right arm forward, pivot your body around on your left foot and flick the ball as it leaves your hand, so that your palm ends up face-down. Spin the ball using your third finger. Make sure the left arm does not drop to the side after you release the ball.

Watch the ball as it pitches and always be ready to take a return catch off your own bowling.

4 As the right arm comes over your head, pivot your body on the left foot. Bring the right arm down and past your left thigh as you complete the action.

31

BOWLING SKILLS

The off-spin

AN OFF-SPIN BOWLER spins the ball so that it changes direction from the off stump to the leg stump after it pitches. The ball moves in the opposite direction to the leg spinner and is usually bowled at a slower speed. Off-spin bowlers have good control over the ball's delivery, but do not achieve as much bounce as leg spinners. They must pitch the ball at just the right length to prevent the batters from scoring runs.

Off-spin bowling

The off-spin bowler aims the ball just outside the off stump so that when it turns the ball will hit the wickets and dismiss the batter. The run-up for off-spinners is usually much shorter than for fast bowlers and it is helpful to run at a slight angle to the popping crease. This helps you to keep your sideways-on position as you deliver the ball.

The off-spin grip

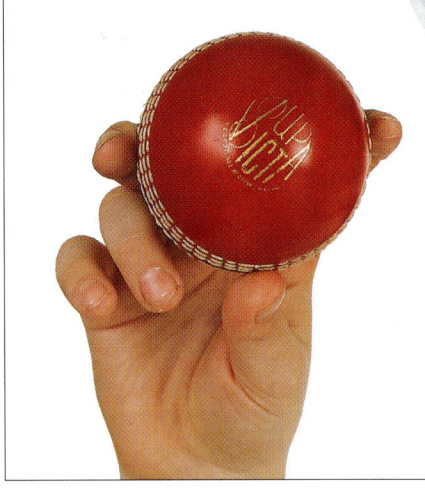

Hold the ball with the seam in a vertical position. Spread your first and second fingers across the top of the ball on the seam, using your third finger and thumb to support the ball. Use your first finger to put spin on the ball.

2 As you prepare to deliver the ball, slowly start to uncoil your body. Your body weight will gradually shift from your back leg to your front leg.

Cock your wrist back.

Continue to look at your target over your left shoulder.

Use the left arm to maintain your balance as the right arm comes over.

Keep your hips and shoulders in line.

1 As you land on your right foot, lean back. Keep your sideways-on position and look over your left shoulder.

Make sure your right foot is parallel to the crease.

32

THE OFF-SPIN

Your bowling arm should be at 11 o'clock. Aim to slice the batter in half with your left hand as the left arm comes down. This will help straighten the right arm as you release the ball.

Keep your head upright throughout the bowling action.

The perfect follow-through
Pakistan's Saqlain Mushtaq gets the follow-through just right. His body weight is on his toes at maximum elevation, his upper body is erect, and his eyes are following the ball.

Your body should have turned 180° from the pre-delivery position.

Your head remains upright and steady.

4 Swivel your upper body on the left knee as you complete the follow-through. Your bowling arm should complete its action near the right hip.

3 As you release the ball, spin it sharply by moving your first finger downwards and your thumb upwards. Make sure your bowling arm brushes past your right ear as it moves down. Your body will gain momentum as it uncoils and your weight shifts on to the ball of your left foot.

Drive your back knee forwards.

Keep your weight on the ball of your front foot.

Transfer your body weight on to your toes as you follow-through.

FIELDING SKILLS

Wicket-keeping

THE WICKET-KEEPER is rarely the star of a match, yet many players think this is the most challenging position in the game. To be a good wicket-keeper, you need lightning reactions, a sharp eye, and physical stamina. You must be able to catch the last ball of the day with as much skill as the first. Wicket-keeping also demands mental stamina. You need to concentrate for long periods of time and provide encouragement to the bowlers when their confidence is low.

Keep your eyes on the ball at all times and try not to let the batter or bowler distract you. Concentration is everything!

Taking the ball

Take up the basic stance about half a pace behind the wicket and slightly to the batter's offside to give you a clear view of the bowler. Make sure no part of your equipment or body passes the wicket. This position is ideal for spin bowlers and medium-pace bowlers, but you will need to be further behind the wicket for fast bowlers.

1 Keep your eyes on the ball and stay crouched and relaxed. Rise when it bounces, keeping your hands low and fingers pointing downwards.

Pads, gloves, and box are crucial when playing with a hard ball.

Stand on a line parallel to the crease.

Keep your hands together and your palms open.

The basic stance

Crouch with your hands resting on the ground and your feet half your shoulder-width apart. If your feet are too far apart, getting up will be difficult. Your body should feel relaxed but ready to move in an instant.

Bending forwards a little helps you stay balanced.

Keep your head steady.

Keep your hands together, with palms facing forwards and fingers pointing downwards.

Your weight should be on the balls of your feet.

Hands relaxed

34

WICKET-KEEPING

2 If the ball goes down the leg side, step back with your left foot. Step back with your right foot if it goes down the off side.

Keep your hands open to produce a large catching zone.

Step back so that you can turn sideways.

3 Take the ball at stomach height, letting your hands "give" as you catch it. If it bounces high, take it to one side of your body.

Watch the ball all the way into your gloves.

Look for a stumping chance once you have taken the ball.

Keep your body weight forwards.

The stumping chance

Good wicket-keepers anticipate a stumping chance long before it comes their way. Batters may step out to play certain balls if they feel unable to tackle them from within the crease. Watch the batter closely for signs of tiredness or carelessness. Trust your instincts. If you think the batter is outside the crease, go for it.

Stumped!
The Sri Lankan wicket-keeper stumps an Australian batter during the 1996 Cricket World Cup in Lahore, Pakistan.

1 Keep your eyes on the ball as you catch it. Bend your knees to stay flexible.

2 Make sure you have the ball safely in your hands as you move across to the bails.

3 Knock the bails off the stumps as quickly as you can.

Legs bent

FIELDING SKILLS

Fielding basics

THE OLD SAYING "catches win matches" is worth remembering each time your team goes out to field. However, a team's success at fielding is not just dependent on good catching – fast and precise intercepting and retrieving, together with powerful and accurate throwing are just as important. To be a successful fielder, you need to master all these skills and maintain a high level of alertness, concentration, and fitness.

Diving for a catch
South African Jonty Rhodes show his readiness to go for anything as he launches himself across the field in a spectacular one-handed diving catch.

The long barrier

The safest way to stop a ball on the field is to make a wall with your body, but it is fairly time consuming. This method should be used when there is no danger of a batter getting an extra run. It is a defensive fielding skill that all beginners should master.

Your hips and shoulders should face the direction of the ball.

Your head should be in front of the instep of your right foot.

Watch out for unexpected bounce.

1 Move into the line of the approaching ball, placing your right foot at right angles to it. Keep your weight balanced on both feet, and move into a low position ready to receive the ball.

2 As the ball comes in close to you, check that your right foot is in the correct position. Bend your left knee and prepare to retrieve the ball by putting your hands together in front of you.

3 Kneel on your left knee to complete the wall. Watch the ball as it comes into your hands, keeping your fingers together and pointing downwards. Don't pick the ball up until it is directly in front of you.

Close-in catching

When fielding close to the wicket, you should adopt a crouched, ready position. Stand on the balls of your feet with your knees flexed. Make sure your weight is distributed evenly and keep your head up and your eyes level. Be alert at all times.

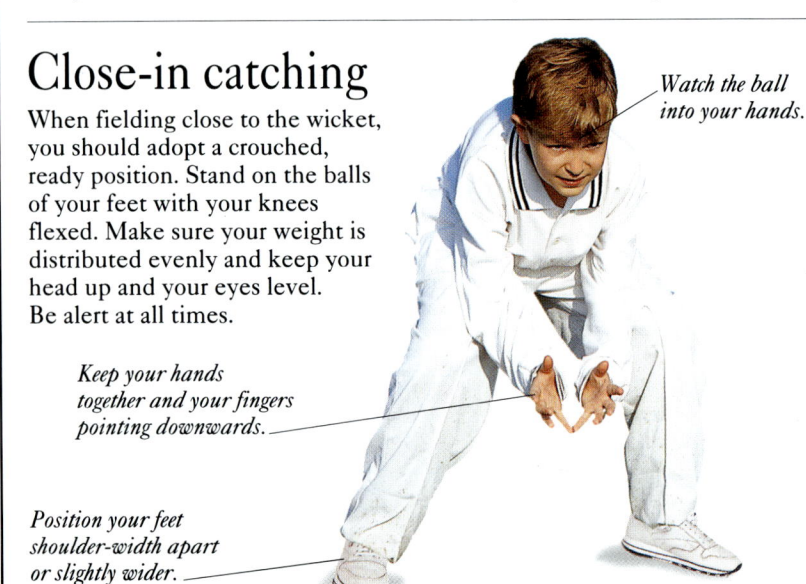

Keep your hands together and your fingers pointing downwards.

Position your feet shoulder-width apart or slightly wider.

Watch the ball into your hands.

Crouched down
Ian Botham demonstrates a crouched catching position in an international match against Pakistan. He is perfectly balanced as he holds out his hands ready to take the ball.

36

FIELDING BASICS

Standing interception

In situations that require maximum speed, you will need to pick up the ball from a standing position. The sequence below shows a two-handed interception. Once you feel confident at retrieving the ball in this way, you should practise intercepting the ball with one hand and throwing it back while you are still moving.

Keep your head still and your eyes level.

1 Move your body slightly to the left of the expected line of the ball. You should have your weight on the balls of your feet as you begin to move into a low position. Make sure you are perfectly balanced.

2 Bend both knees as you prepare to pick up the ball, keeping your hands close together. You start to move into this low position later than you would for the long barrier.

Watch the ball at all times.

Keep your fingers together.

3 Watch the ball as it comes into your hands, keeping a wide stance. Once you make contact with the ball, bring it in towards your chest. Turn to face the direction you want to throw the ball.

Left-handed fielders
All instructions in the book are for right-handed fielders. Try holding a mirror alongside these pictures to see the left-handed positions.

Keep your weight on the balls of your feet.

Overarm throwing

It is more important for beginners to throw accurately than with power or speed. Practise throwing from a variety of positions on the field. Underarm throws are only used when you are close to the wicket.

1 Stand sideways-on to the wicket you are aiming at and place your weight on your back foot. Bring your right hand back behind your shoulder and point your non-throwing arm at the target. For very long throws, extend your right arm out fully.

Your elbow should be level with your shoulder.

Bend your knees slightly.

Your right foot should be at right angles to the line of throw.

2 Bring your right arm over in line with the target, shifting your body weight from the back leg to the front leg. Complete the action by swinging the right arm down in front of your body.

Pivot your body on the front foot and lean forwards as you release the ball.

FIELDING SKILLS

Fielding activities

ALTHOUGH PLAYERS tend to specialize in certain fielding positions (see pages 10–11), the best fielders have excellent all-round fielding skills. The activities on these pages show ways you can develop a range of fielding techniques safely and effectively. It is a good idea to practise them on a regular basis – all you need is a tennis ball, a wall, stumps, and some other keen players.

How to catch

Fielders positioned in the outfield (near the boundary line) often have to take high catches. It is important to remember that a ball coming at high speed could cause injury to your fingers if you don't catch it in the correct way. Practise throwing and catching the ball as much as you can.

The right way
Cup your hands together with your fingers pointing away from you. Keep your elbows clear of your body. Catch the ball at eye level or above, and draw it in close to you.

Keep your eyes on the ball at all times.

Your elbows should help to cushion the impact of the catch.

Close catching

You will need two fielders for this activity. One player takes up a ready position behind the wicket, standing with feet shoulder-width apart. The other player throws the ball, bouncing it up to each side of the wicket. Aim to bounce the ball about 3 m (10 ft) from the stumps. Swap positions after 10 catches.

Off stump

Leg stump

Cup your hands ready to catch the ball.

1 Your partner throws the ball to the off side of the wicket. Step back on to your right foot, bending your knees and keeping your eyes on the ball. Keep your elbows clear of your body and your fingers pointing downwards as you catch the ball. Throw the ball back to your partner after each catch.

2 This time, your partner throws the ball to the leg side of the wicket. Step back on to your left foot, bending your knees again and keeping your eyes on the ball. Keep your elbows clear of your body and your hands in the correct catching position.

Your little fingers should be touching each other.

For paired or group activities, take it in turns to throw, catch, and retrieve the ball.

Try to stay balanced as you step back to take the ball.

Throwing

Attach a balloon to the middle stump and stand about 10 m (32 ft) away from it. Aim a tennis ball at the centre of the balloon. As you improve, move further away from the target.

38

FIELDING ACTIVITIES

Be careful not to spread your fingers too far.

The wrong way
Avoid catching a ball with your fingers spread out in this way. They can easily get caught under the ball and be injured. The elbows here are too close to the body.

See how many catches you can make in one minute.

Try using different types of ball.

Rebound catch
You will need two fielders for this activity. Player B takes up a close-catching position about 3 m (10 ft) from a wall. Player A stands behind player B slightly to one side. Player A throws the ball against the wall at eye level and player B catches it and hands it back.

Running pick-up, throw, and catch
You will need three or more players for this activity. Player B rolls a ball gently so that it doesn't bounce along the ground. Player A chases after the ball, retrieves it, and throws it back to player B, who is still in line. Player C then takes the ball and rolls it out for player B. The first fielder goes to the back of the line. As you improve, try rolling different types of ball at different speeds.

1 Lean forwards with your legs slightly bent as player B releases the ball. Chase after the ball.

Bend your knees as you release the ball.

The ball should travel in a straight line.

2 As you approach the ball, make sure it is on the outside of your right foot. Bend low and pick up the ball in your right hand.

Keep your eyes on the ball at all times.

You should be in a crouched position ready to catch the ball.

Keep your weight on the balls of your feet.

3 Turn in an anticlockwise direction to face the other players. Throw the ball back, bouncing it 1–2 m (3–6 ft) in front of player B.

Keep your elbow level with your shoulder.

Aim your non-throwing arm at the target.

Keep your weight on your back foot.

Your hands give as you catch the ball.

OTHER EVENTS

Taking it further

CRICKET, WHEN PLAYED at the highest level, is all about believing in yourself. All serious players know the basics well enough, they have natural talent, and they work hard to stay fit. However, it is your ability to cope with pressure and play in difficult conditions that will decide whether you are cut out for competition or just playing the game for fun. Either way, what is most important is that you get pleasure from playing cricket. Most top players who perform well in major international matches admit that the sheer joy of being in the game helps them cope with the pressure.

Street cricketers playing against a makeshift wicket in Guyana.

Where to start
If you enjoy playing cricket and want to join a team, find out where you can get proper coaching and play matches of a high standard. In most countries, cricket is organized by clubs and schools. It is also organized by age – from under-12 sides to inter-university competitions. Find out more about the cricket-friendly schools in your area. Also, check to see if your local club holds trials for your age group, and if they have winter or summer training camps.

Two young players hone their batting and wicket-keeping skills.

Street cricket
In Asia, Africa, and the Caribbean, streets serve as natural playing grounds for young cricketers. Proper gear and training are often unavailable, yet nothing dampens the players' enthusiasm for the game. Many of the well-known names in cricket today – like Sachin Tendulkar and Brian Lara – picked up their early cricketing skills while playing on neighbourhood streets.

Kwik criket
Kwik criket began in England in the 1980s and quickly caught on in other countries, such as New Zealand. This scheme promotes the game among children in the 8–13 age group. The children are allowed to play at first-class and Test venues during lunch and tea breaks. They use a special rubber ball that swings and turns like a normal cricket ball, but is too soft to cause injuries.

TAKING IT FURTHER

Fans participate
Today, cricket fans the world over flock to the ground not merely to watch a match, but to be part of an event. National flags fly high, there are competitions for the best banners, and "Mexican waves" make their way around the ground. Many fans paint their faces in their team's colours.

The impact of television
TV coverage means that fans no longer need to be at the stadium to feel involved in a match. Most international TV channels cover the major tournaments, using up to 13 cameras to broadcast a cricket final live. Special "spin vision" cameras give high-resolution, slow-motion pictures. More recently, TV cameras have been used to help the umpires. In international matches, for example, a third umpire sits in a special room where he can keep a close eye on the action on screen.

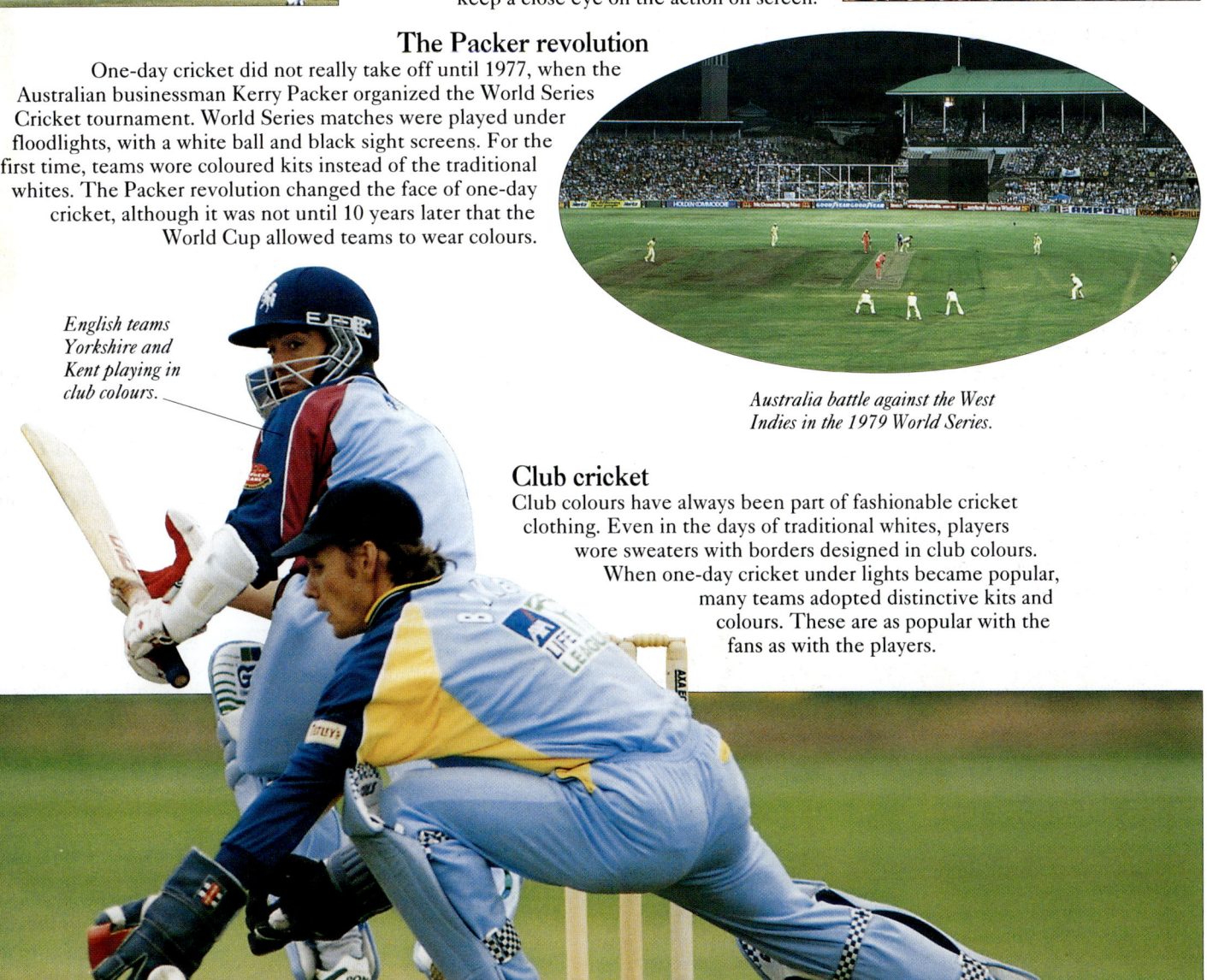

The Packer revolution
One-day cricket did not really take off until 1977, when the Australian businessman Kerry Packer organized the World Series Cricket tournament. World Series matches were played under floodlights, with a white ball and black sight screens. For the first time, teams wore coloured kits instead of the traditional whites. The Packer revolution changed the face of one-day cricket, although it was not until 10 years later that the World Cup allowed teams to wear colours.

English teams Yorkshire and Kent playing in club colours.

Australia battle against the West Indies in the 1979 World Series.

Club cricket
Club colours have always been part of fashionable cricket clothing. Even in the days of traditional whites, players wore sweaters with borders designed in club colours. When one-day cricket under lights became popular, many teams adopted distinctive kits and colours. These are as popular with the fans as with the players.

OTHER EVENTS

Tournaments and competitions

CRICKET HAS EVOLVED over the years, with the traditional five-day format changing in the late 1960s to accommodate one-day matches. The game has also become more popular and diverse, with women and the visually impaired now playing in international competitions. Recently, the International Cricket Council (ICC) – a body that governs the game internationally – has begun making plans for a world Test cricket championship.

Test cricket
The most prestigious form of international cricket is Test cricket. Test matches last five days, and are played only between the official Test nations. These are Australia, England, India, New Zealand, Pakistan, South Africa, Sri Lanka, West Indies (a consortium of Caribbean countries), and Zimbabwe. Opposing sides play a set of up to six matches – a Test series. The most famous Test series is the Ashes.

West Indies players celebrate a wicket in a Test match against England.

The modern Ashes trophy is made of glass.

The original Ashes urn

The Ashes
In 1882, England lost an international series for the first time to a touring Australian side. The next day, a mock obituary appeared in the *Sporting Times*, mourning "the death of English cricket". A pair of cricket bails were burnt and the ashes placed in a small urn, which was presented to the Australian captain to be taken back as a trophy. What was meant as a joke soon became a part of cricket history. Since then, England and Australia have battled for "the Ashes" every two years.

Women's cricket
Women's cricket is not as widely followed as men's, although the women's World Cup began two years before the men's, and increasing numbers of girls are joining clubs. England hosted and won the first women's World Cup in 1973, defended the trophy four years later when the event took place in India, and won again in 1993. Australia were trophy holders in 1982, 1988, and 1997.

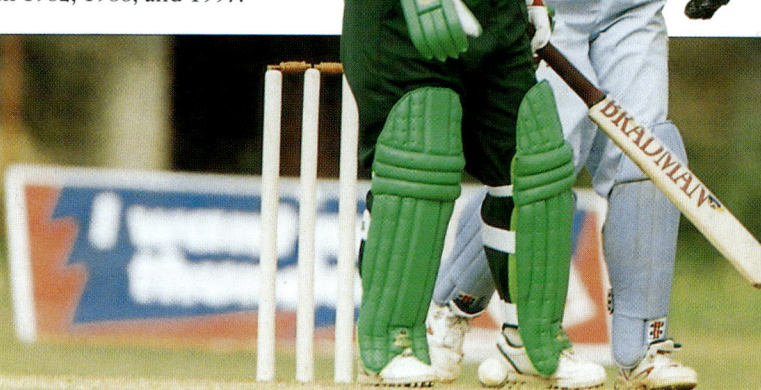

England's Jane Cassar appeals for lbw at a 1997 World Cup match against Pakistan.

Cricket for the blind
The first World Cup for the blind took place in India in November 1998. As well as the host team, there were teams from England, Australia, New Zealand, South Africa, Pakistan, and Sri Lanka. In cricket for the blind, a special hollow ball filled with bells is used so that the players can hear it coming. The ball must be bowled underarm so that it rolls along the ground instead of bouncing off the pitch. The fielding positions are different to normal cricket. For example, some fielders stand very close to the batter and wait for the ball to come towards them along the ground.

42

TOURNAMENTS AND COMPETITIONS

World Cup winners
The world's biggest cricket championship – the World Cup – takes place every four years. All the Test-playing countries take part in it. In addition, two or three qualifiers from the ICC Trophy (played every four years) also take part. Unlike Test cricket, the World Cup consists of one-day matches. Players wear team colours and can use a white ball, instead of the traditional red. Here, Australia celebrate their first World Cup victory in 1987, led by captain Allan Border.

New Zealand and England line up at a Cricket Max tournament.

Imran Khan lifts the World Cup trophy after Pakistan's 1992 defeat of England.

Cricket Max
The first Cricket Max game took place in New Zealand in 1996. Cricket Max is a shortened form of the game designed for TV coverage. Matches are only three hours long, each team playing two innings of 10 overs. Fewer no-balls are allowed than in Test cricket, and the field has a special "max zone" at either end. Batters can double their runs by playing balls into the max zones.

Leading from the front
Under the shrewd captaincy of Imran Khan, Pakistan lifted the World Cup in 1992 after struggling to qualify for the quarter finals at one stage. Imran, who decided to retire from the game after winning the crystal trophy, rarely bowled in this tournament but made crucial runs. He was fortunate to have a very strong team, which included the phenomenal talents of Wasim Akram, Javed Miandad, and Inzaman-ul Haq.

At the Commonwealth Games
Cricket was made part of the Commonwealth Games for the first time in 1998. Ironically, England decided against sending a team for the tournament. All matches were played on a newly laid turf at the Pedang in the heart of Kuala Lumpur, Malaysia. South African captain Hansie Cronje led his team to victory and won the gold medal.

GLOSSARY

Glossary

A
Appeal When the fielding side think the batter is out and appeal to the umpire to consider the dismissal of the batter by shouting "Howzat".

B
Back-foot attack An attack shot played to balls that pitch a long way in front of the batter, either side of the stumps.

Back-foot defence A defensive batting shot played to a straight ball that pitches short.

Backswing The initial movement of the bat as the batter raises it backwards and then swings it forwards to play the ball.

Block The mark made by the batter inside the popping crease to indicate the position of the guard.

Bodyline An aggressive bowling strategy in which the ball bounces up towards the batter's upper body, forcing the batter to hit the ball high.

Coaching ball

Boundary line The edge of the field of play, marked by a rope, flags, or line.

Bowled out When a batter misses the ball and it hits and breaks the wicket directly from the bowler's delivery, or if the ball hits the wicket after deflecting off the bat or the batter's body.

Bowling crease The lines on the pitch along which the stumps are positioned.

Bowling mark A mark on the field made by the bowler at the start of the run-up, to make sure that the bowler always runs from the same place.

Break The change of direction of the ball from a straight line after it hits the pitch.

Breaking the wicket When one or both of the bails on the wicket is dislodged by the ball and falls to the ground.

Bye A run scored after the batter misses the ball and the wicket-keeper fails to stop it.

C
Century A hundred runs scored by a single batter in one innings.

Chucking An illegal style of bowling in which the bowler's arm straightens as he delivers the ball.

Close field An attacking fielding strategy where fielders stand close to the batter.

Cover region The fielding area located on the off side close to the batter where fielders take catches and stop batters from getting single runs.

Cover drive An attack stroke towards the off side, played to balls in line with or just outside the off stump.

Cut A shot made at a short-pitched ball on the off side.

D
Danger area The area, 1.2 m (4 ft) in front of the popping crease and 0.6 m (2 ft) across, into which the bowler is not meant to follow through.

Dead ball A ball that is out of play, for example when the batter is out.

Declaration A captain's decision to finish a team's innings before all wickets are lost.

Deep point Fielding positions away from the pitch near to the boundary.

The square cut

The pitch

Drive A batting stroke made with a full downward swing of the bat.

Duck When the batter is dismissed without getting any runs. If you are out on your first ball, you are out for a "golden duck".

E
Extras Runs made without the batter hitting the ball with the bat. They can be made by wide balls, no-balls, byes, and leg byes.

Wicket-keeping

F
Fine leg A fielding position on the leg side, which stops a fine deflection from the bat.

Flick A type of shot that deflects balls behind the wicket and on to the leg side.

Fly slip The fielding position between the third slip and the third man on the boundary.

Follow-on rule In a two-innings match, the rule allowing the second team to bat again if they are losing by a specified number of runs.

Forward defence A defensive form of batting used against balls that pitch in line with the wicket at good length.

Four A score of four runs automatically awarded when the ball travels across the boundary line after having bounced inside it.

Full pitch/toss A delivery that reaches the batter without touching the ground first.

G
Given out Generally when a batter is bowled or caught out and he or she has to leave the field.

Glance A ball deflected off the face of the bat to a fine leg.

44

Glossary

Good length A ball that bounces at a distance that makes it difficult for the batter to decide whether to move forwards or backwards to hit it.

Googly A trick ball, bowled by a leg-spin bowler, that spins the opposite way from the direction the batter is expecting.

Guard The batter's preferred position in front of the wicket, usually somewhere between middle and leg stump.

Gully A catching position just square of the batter, on the off side of the field.

H
Half-volley A ball which bounces just before the batter – usually very easy to hit.

Handling the ball When a batter illegally obstructs the ball with the hand.

Hat trick When a bowler gets three wickets from three consecutive balls any time in a match.

Head and shoulder lead A movement of the head and shoulders that puts the body and feet into a good position to play a shot.

Hitting the ball twice When the batter is declared out for making contact with the ball a second time.

Hitting the wicket When the batter knocks the wicket (with the bat or feet), causing the bails to fall off, and is out.

Hook A back-foot shot played towards leg side when the ball bounces at shoulder height.

"Howzat" A term shouted by the fielding team when they think the batter should be given out.

Warming up

I
Innings The period of play when a team bats, ending when all wickets have fallen or the captain "declares". In Test matches each team plays two innings, and in one-day matches each team plays a single innings.

Inserting the opposition When, on winning the toss, a captain decides that his or her team will field first and invites the opposition to bat.

Inswinger A delivery that "swings" (moves) towards the batter while in mid-air.

L
Lbw (leg before wicket) When the batter deliberately uses the body to stop the ball hitting the wicket, the umpire may rule the batter out lbw.

Leg bye A run a batter makes after accidentally deflecting the ball with the body.

Leg side The half of the cricket field behind the batter, also known as "on side".

Leg spinner A bowling technique that turns the ball from the leg stump towards the middle and off stumps.

Leg stump One of the three wicket stumps; the leg stump is nearest the "on side" (leg side).

Length of the ball The distance between the batter and the point where the ball pitches after it has been bowled.

Limited-over match A match where the number of overs is agreed before the start of the match.

Line of the ball The direction in which the ball moves towards the stumps after pitching on the ground.

M
Maiden over A complete over where the batter fails to score any runs and there are no wide balls or no-balls bowled.

Mid-off/mid-on Fielding positions intended to catch batting strokes called drives.

Mid wicket A fielding position between square leg and mid-on.

N
No-ball A delivery that the umpire considers unfair. Another ball is bowled and the batting team gets an extra run.

Not out When a batter is still playing at the end of an innings.

O
Obstructing the field When the batter wilfully obstructs the wicket-keeper or a fielder, and is declared out.

Off-break delivery A delivery that pitches and turns from the off side to the leg side.

Off side The half of the cricket field opposite to the leg side.

Off stump One of the three wicket stumps. The off stump is furthest away from the batter.

On drive A batting shot that sends the ball to the on side. It is played against balls that are in line with or outside the leg stump.

On side Another name for leg side.

Outfield The part of the field that is not the pitch.

Outswinger A delivery that "swings" (moves) away from the batter, towards the off side, while in the air.

Over The bowler's six consecutive balls to the batter.

Overthrow When a fielder throws the ball past the wicket-keeper allowing the batters to run again.

P
Pace bowling The technique adopted by fast bowlers who rely on speed.

Popping crease The crease line parallel and in front of the bowling crease and wicket. It is the edge of the batter's safety zone and the line the batter needs to reach to score a run.

Pre-delivery

Bat

Wicket stumps and bails

45

GLOSSARY

Pull A batting shot that sends the ball to the leg side, played to a short ball outside the leg stump.

R
Return creases Lines drawn between the bowling and popping creases. Bowlers must bowl from between the two return creases.

Fielding

Rhythm The development of a consistent backswing, which enables a good shot to be played.

Run out If the wicket-keeper removes a bail while holding the ball, and the batter is still outside the popping crease during a run, then the batter is run out.

Runner A substitute runner brought on to do the running if a batter is injured and unable to run between wickets.

S
Sight screen A screen set up opposite the batter, outside the boundary, giving a clear background against which to see the ball.

Silly point A catching position in front of the batter on the off side, usually placed for a leg- or left-arm spinner, to put pressure on the batter.

Six A score of six runs automatically awarded when the ball is hit beyond the boundary without bouncing first.

Slip A close-in, catching field position on the off side, behind the batter. The slip region can contain up to four fielders to make up the slip cordon.

Slip cordon Fielding area behind the wicket on the off side, where fielders catch balls that come off the edge of the bat.

Slog overs The last ten overs in a limited-overs match. During these, the batting side stops paying too much attention to losing further wickets. Instead, it takes risks to get as many runs as possible.

Spin bowling The technique adopted by bowlers who are slower in pace, but who turn or twist the ball, making it change direction when it pitches.

Spinner A bowler who rotates the ball with the fingers or wrist, so that it changes direction after pitching.

Square boundary The fielding area at right angles to the line of the pitch, on the popping crease, and located on both the off side and on side.

Square cut A batting stroke made off the back foot to a short delivery just outside the off stump.

Preparing to bat

Straight drive A powerful attack stroke that sends the ball directly towards the bowler.

Stumping When a wicket-keeper dislodges a bail with the ball in his hand, and the batter does not have the bat or part of the body behind the popping crease.

Sweep A batting stroke that sends the ball to the on side with a horizontal sweeping movement of the bat. It is played to good length balls that pitch in line with or outside the leg stump.

Sweeper A fielding position situated in the cover region on the off side. The fielder moves between deep point and mid-off, depending on the type of bowler.

Swing of the ball The movement of the ball in the air after it leaves the bowler's hand before and after it pitches on the ground.

T
Taking guard When the batter decides where to stand in relation to the stumps.

Third man A fielding position behind the slips on the off side that cuts out possible fours when the batter edges the ball through the slips.

Timed-out Rare type of dismissal intended to prevent time-wasting by the batting side.

Toss When the captains of both teams toss a coin in the presence of the umpire at the start of the game. The winner of the toss can choose to bat or bowl first.

Twelfth man The officially appointed substitute when the captains exchange team lists at the beginning of the match.

W
Wide ball A ball that is unplayable because it is pitched beyond the batter's reach. An extra ball is delivered and the batter gets a run. If the batter tries to hit the ball, no wide is allowed.

Y
Yorker A long ball that is pitched at the batter's feet.

Wicket-keeper's gloves

Groin stretch

Useful addresses

Here are the addresses of some important cricket associations that you can contact.

West Indies Cricket Board of Control (WICBC)
Factory Road, PO Box 616 W
Woods Centre
St John's
Antigua

The Australian Cricket Board (ACB)
90 Jolimont Street
Jolimont
Victoria 3002
Australia
Website: www.acb.com.au

QLD Junior Cricket Association Inc.
PO Box 575
Albion QLD 4010
Australia
E-mail: terrywalsh@ultra.net.au

Coach Education Department England and Wales Cricket Board
Warwickshire County Cricket Club
Edgbaston
Birmingham B5 7QX
England

The England and Wales Cricket Board
Lord's Cricket Ground
St Johns Wood
London
NW8 8QN
England

6. **The International Cricket Council (ICC)**
Lord's Cricket Ground
St Johns Wood
London NW8 8QN
England
Website: www.lords.org

7. **Middlesex County Cricket Club**
Phil Knappet
The Academy
East End Road
London N3 2TA
England

8. **Association of Cricket Statisticians and Scorers of India (ACSSI)**
Post Box No 7145
Wadala Post Office
Bombay 400 041
India

9. **Association for Promotion of Cricket for the Blind**
George Abraham, President
E 62 Jalvayu Vihar
Sector 21
Noida 201301
India
E-mail: geham@ndb.vsnl.net.in

10. **Board of Control for Cricket in India (BCCI)**
Randhir Singh Mahendra
Vijay Nagar Colony
Bhiwani 125021
Haryana
India

11. **New Zealand Cricket Council**
PO Box 958
Christchurch
New Zealand

12. **Pakistan Cricket Board (PCB)**
Majid Khan
The Gaddafi Stadium
Ferozepur Road
Lahore 54600
Pakistan

13. **United Cricket Board of South Africa**
Wanderers Club
North Street
Illovo
PO Box 55009
Northlands 2116
Republic of South Africa

14. **Board of Control for Cricket in Sri Lanka (BCCSL)**
Dhammika Ranatunga
35 Maitland Place
Colombo 7
Sri Lanka

Index

Ashes 42

Back-foot attack 22-23, 44
back-foot defence 17, 44
backswing 15, 44
bails 6, 35
balls 6
   catching 36, 38-39
   grip 27-30, 32
   throwing 37
   wicket-keeping 34-35
bats 6
batting 14-25
   back-foot attack 22-23
   back-foot defence 17, 44
   being out 12-13
   defensive strokes 16-17
   drives 18-19
   equipment 7
   hook, pull, and flick 24-25
   on drive 20
   preparation 14-15
   square cut 22-23
   sweep 21
blind cricket 42
block 44
bodyline bowling 5, 44
Botham, Ian 36
bouncers 23, 24
boundary line 11, 44
bowling 10, 26-33
   bodyline bowling 5
   run-up 26-27
   spin bowling 30-33, 46
   swing bowling 28-29
Bradman, Donald 5
byes 12, 44

Cassar, Jane 42
catching 36, 38-39
chest pads 7
clothes 7
club cricket 41
Commonwealth Games 43
competitions 42-43
cover drive 18-19
creases 12, 44
Cricket Max 43
Cronje, Hansie 18, 43

Defensive strokes 16-17
Donald, Allan 27
drives 18-20, 44

Elbow guards 7
equipment 6-7
exercises, warming up 8-9

Fielding 10, 11, 36-39
flick 24, 25, 44
forward defence 16-17

Gloves 6, 7
Grace, Dr W.G. 5
grip
   ball 27-30, 32
   bat 14
guards 7

Helmets 7
history 5
hook shot 24-25, 45

Innings 10, 45
inswinger 28, 45

International Cricket Council (ICC) 42

Jadeja, Ajay 4, 24
Jardine, Douglas 5
junior cricket 6

Khan, Imran 43
Kwik cricket 40

Leg glance 24, 25
leg-spin bowling 30-31
Lord's Cricket Ground 10, 11

Marylebone Cricket Club (MCC) 10, 12
matches 40-43
Moody, Tom 16
Mushtaq, Saqlain 33

Off-spin bowling 32-33
on drive 20, 45
one-day cricket 5
outswinger 29, 45
overarm throwing 37

Packer, Kerry 41
pads 7
pitch 10, 11
popping crease 12, 45
protective equipment 7
pull shot 24-25

Rhodes, Jonty 36
rules 12-13
runs 10
run-up, bowling 26-27

Scoreboards 10
scoring 10
shoes 6, 7
signals, umpires 12-13
spin bowling 30-33, 46
Stewart, Alec 4
straight drive 19
street cricket 40
stretching exercises 8-9
strokes, batting 16-19
stumping 35, 46
stumps 6
substitutes 10
sun protection 6
sweep 21, 46
swing bowling 28-29

Taking guard 14, 46
television 41
Test matches 42
thigh pads 7
throwing overarm 37
toss 10, 46
tournaments 42-43

Umpires 10, 12-13

Warming up 8-9
Warne, Shane 6, 31
Waugh, Mark 22
Waugh, Steve 21
wicket-keeping 6, 34-35
wickets, ways of being out 12-13
women's cricket 42
World Cup 43
World Series 41

Acknowledgments

Dorling Kindersley would like to thank the following people for their kind help in the production of this book:

R. P. Sharma, cricket coach, for his technical advice and help during photo shoots; all the young cricketers for their patience and good humour during the photography, and also their families; Mr Garg for his cooperation; Reebok India Company for supplying the cricket clothes and equipment; Piers Tilbury for designing the book jacket; managing art editor Rachael Foster; Rebecca Johns and Carole Oliver for design assistance; Robin Hunter for producing the cricket diagrams; managing editor Mary Ling; Sue Leonard, Jonathan Percy, Amanda Rayner, Fiona Robertson, Lee Simmons, and Selina Wood for editorial assistance; Hilary Bird for preparing the index.

Picture credits:
The publisher would like to thank the following for their kind permission to reproduce their photographs:

Key:
t=top, b=below, l=left, r=right, c=centre.
Allsport: 41tr, 43cr, 43bl; Shaun Botterill 12cr; Stu Foster 41tl; Laurence Griffiths 4br, 41b; Hulton Deutsch 5cra, 5bl; Clive Mason 4cl; Stephen Munday 42cl; Craig Prentis 42cr; Mark Thomas 4cr.
Colorsport: 5c, 11tc.
Patrick Eagar Photography: 4tr, 5br, 35cr, 36tr, 41cr, 43tl.
Mary Evans Picture Library: 5tc.
Pradeep Mandhani, Fotomedia: 4bl, 6tr, 10cr, 16tr, 18tr, 21tr, 22tr, 24tr, 27tr, 33tc, 40bl, 43br, 72bl.
Sporting Pictures (UK) Ltd: 10cl, 36br, 40c; Jeff Dujon 42tr; M. Rayner 40tr.
Jacket credits:
Front jacket: Allsport: Phil Cole tl.
Patrick Eagar: bl.
Back jacket: Colorsport: bcl.
Pradeep Mandhani: bcr.